31

DAYS OF

Mountaintop Miracles

*One Woman's Legacy of
Unconditional Obedience*

from the Founder of Operation Care International

SUSIE Y. JENNINGS, RN

with Allison Bottke

Clovercroft Publishing

31 Days of Mountaintop Miracles:
One Woman's Legacy of Unconditional Obedience

©2014 by Susie Y. Jennings, RN
Third Edition

Co-published by Clovercroft Publishing, Franklin, Tennessee (www.clovercroft-publishing.com) and Roaring Lambs Publishing, Dallas, Texas (www.RoaringLambs.org). Published in association with Larry Carpenter of Christian Book Services, LLC. www.christianbookservices.com

Edited by Allison Bottke
Cover and Interior Layout Design by Suzanne Lawing
Cover Photograph by James Gates

Printed in the United States of America

978-1-940262-83-3

In Praise of *31 Days of Mountaintop Miracles* ...

Susie Jennings is a true servant of God whose life was transformed from tragedy to triumph after the sudden death of her husband. When Susie chose to obey God unconditionally and fully rely on Him, God met her needs in amazing and miraculous ways. In *31 Days of Mountaintop Miracles* it is clear to see the mighty hand of God on Susie's life as she walks in love and obedience to Him. Readers will be inspired and encouraged to look at life through the lens of faith to see the miracles God provides.

—**Dr. Robert Jeffress**, Senior Pastor, First Baptist Church, Dallas, TX

Susie Jennings is the real deal and a miracle in and of herself. Take this 31-day journey with her and you will be challenged to see what God can do with one person... YOU...who is totally sold out to Him! Read it and reap!

—**Dr. O.S. Hawkins**, President/CEO, Guidestone Financial Resources

For more than a decade, it has been my privilege to serve along Susie as her Aaron, and see firsthand why God blesses Operation Care International, especially through miracles. It's because of Susie's unwavering commitment in her leadership to three basic tenants: 1) Total belief in and dependence on the power of prayer, 2) Unconditional obedience without compromise to God's will and His Word, and 3) To always give God the Glory and to praise Him in both the good times and the hard times. This is how a humble leader has accomplished great things—this is the "secret" to her success.

—**Ron Batts**, President, Prepared 4 Life, and Chairman of the Board, Operation Care International

Susie is a remarkable lady who not only believes in miracles but has experienced them over and over. Operation Care is likewise a remarkable ministry. If anyone is looking for ROI when investing in a ministry, you need look no further. Unbelievable what this ministry accomplishes with the amount of resources it receives! Get on board with Operation Care and receive tremendous blessings.

—A.C. MUSGRAVE, CHAIRMAN OF THE BOARD, PETRA CHEMICAL COMPANY

Encouragement and empowerment explode on each page as Susie's faith invokes God's faithfulness! The Hebrew word for bless is "baruch" and for knee is "berek" which indicates that to bless, one must bow. There's no better example of this word picture than Susie kneeling in prayer as a blessing to God, and then as a servant to bless others. Enlightening!

—DR. VICTORIA SARVADI, THD, CO-FOUNDER, THE NATHANIEL FOUNDATION

Susie Jennings is one of the most amazing women I've seen. She has a heart for the hurting and homeless of the world. She is an expletory example of a true hero to mankind as she lays her life down and expects nothing in return. Susie Jennings is a true global humanitarian.

—DR. CLYDE RIVERS, NORTH AMERICAN REPRESENTATIVE, INTERFAITH PEACE – BUILDING INITIATIVE TO THE UNITED NATIONS

Susie Jennings' story inspires faith to all who read *31 Days of Mountaintop Miracles*. This is a true account of one woman who influenced nations by her unconditional obedience to God.

—SUELLEN ROBERTS, FOUNDER/PRESIDENT CHRISTIAN WOMEN IN MEDIA

The stories of God's goodness and power, demonstrated in the lives of His people, increase our faith. Susie Jennings brings us story after story of God's faithfulness and miracles, not only in her life but also in the lives of those she has touched. Susie's love for Jesus shines brightly through her life and through her words. As you read this book, may your faith grow and your sense of God's love increase so that you may inspire the lives of those around you.

—**KAROL LADD**, BESTSELLING AUTHOR OF *BECOMING A WOMAN OF THE WORD*

In reading *31 Days of Mountaintop Miracles*, you will see the mighty hand of God in Susie Jennings' life. Her unconditional obedience requires that she move on God's commands, whether or not she knows how He is to accomplish His will. See how God wants to do miraculous things in your life...for His purpose and His glory.

—**RONALD L. HARRIS**, PRESIDENT AND FOUNDER, MEDIA ALLIANCE INTERNATIONAL AND ADVISORY BOARD MEMBER FOR OCI

It is my honor to know Susie Jennings and to watch God do great and mighty things through this little lady. After encouraging her to write down these amazing stories, I am so thrilled that she can now share them with you. I highly recommend that you read this book and see what God wants to do through your life!

—**DONNA SKELL**, EXECUTIVE DIRECTOR, ROARING LAMBS MINISTRIES

There is no greater champion of unconditional obedience than Susie Jennings. The stories in *31 Days of Mountaintop Miracles* will inspire you to step out in faith and encourage you to look at life through a divine perspective.

—**TRACEY MITCHELL**, D.D., TV HOST AND AUTHOR OF *DOWNSIDE UP*

The power of Susie's miracle testimonies shows God's loving care and Susie's faithfulness to Him. You will be astonished and amazed when you see God's power in her life and encouraged to know He cares for you too!

—Dr. Thelma Wells, M. Min. D.D. (Mama T), President of A Woman of God Ministries and That A Girl and Friends Speakers Agency

Susie Jennings is a woman of courage and deep faith, a trophy of God's Grace. Her stories will grip your heart. In this amazing book, you will see the fingerprint of God. Susie not only loves God and His Word, she also deeply loves the unlovable. Susie's servant heart and passion for prayer is beautifully illustrated on every page of *31 Days of Mountaintop Miracles*. Enjoy!

—Sharon Hill, Founder, OnCallPrayer.org, Author of the *On Call Prayer Journal*

Susie Jennings is one of those rare individuals who truly understand the importance of unconditional obedience. She has the purest heart and thinking of anyone I have ever encountered. Susie is totally committed to the high calling on her life. When God speaks, she immediately says, "Yes, Lord." And miracles happen!

—Brenda Mahon, CLU, ChFC, The M Group/ Trinity Portfolio Advisors, LLC

There is no greater testimony to God's love and grace than witnessing one of His awesome miracle moments—the kind that takes your breath away. In *31 Days of Mountaintop Miracles*, we get a front-row seat at a life filled with dozens of these supernatural moments. Experiencing Susie Jennings' world of unconditional obedience is an inspiring journey. Learning to view life from a miracle-minded perspective can change your life—it has surely changed mine.

—Allison Bottke, Bestselling Author of the *Setting Boundaries®* series

The accounts of God's wonderful works in the life of His servant, Susie Jennings, prove that the journey from the valley of pain and despair to the mountaintop is paved with the promises, presence, and power of God. *31 Days of Mountaintop Miracles* is running over with evidence of what unconditional obedience to God and His word will do, by God's divine power, to change a life, affect a culture, and touch the world.

—**WILLIAM THOMPSON**, EXECUTIVE DIRECTOR - UNION GOSPEL MISSION, DALLAS, TX

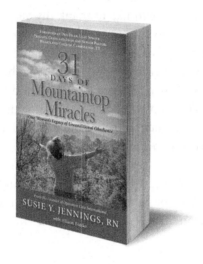

Acknowledgments

It is impossible to list all of the people whose love, encouragement, support and prayers have helped me to reach this place of service. My deepest apologies if I have neglected anyone. I pray that you will know who you are and how very grateful I am to all of you.

First I would like to thank my Jesus for saving me and being my Lord and Savior.

Secondly, I would like to thank my very gifted editor, Allison Bottke for her remarkable editing skills and patience with me as a novice author. Thanking God for all my family, prayer partners, Board Members, Advisory Board, staff, partners, church family, and volunteers of Operation Care International. Without your help and unconditional obedience to our Lord and Savior, I would not be here writing this book.

Last but surely not least, to all the homeless and impoverished children, because of YOU I found purpose.

Thank you for being with me in this miraculous journey of unconditional obedience.

Susie

We've all had a lifetime of miracle moments—the key is to recognize them and give all honor and praise to God for the glorious ways He provides them.
~ Susie Jennings

In Loving Memory

David Jennings – Dear Husband

Betty Yanson – Dear Mother

Eulalio Yanson – Dear Father

Mercy Yanson – Dear Sister

Dr. W.A. Criswell – Dear Pastor

The Miracle of Unconditional Obedience

And now, Israel, what does the LORD your God ask of you but to fear the LORD your God, to walk in obedience to him, to love him, to serve the LORD your God with all your heart and with all your soul, and to observe the LORD's commands …

Deuteronomy 10:12-13 (NIV)

Contents

The Canton Bridge, Downtown Dallas
where I heard the voice of God!

Becky Dean, Susie and Pastor Dan Dean.

Foreword

The Bible has much to say about obedience. One early lesson in scripture came via the authoritative voice of the prophet Samuel, who informed the first King of Israel, "Obedience is better than sacrifice." There are priorities when it comes to doing good things and obedience is at the top of the list. Many times, obedience is costly. Radical, unconditional obedience will require blind faith that only the most devoted soldiers can follow.

When the commanding officer gives the orders to advance, the best soldiers, regardless of their feelings, march forward with little thought to their own safety and survival. What matters is the objective and the discipline to understand rank and authority.

Susie Jennings is one of those special soldiers in God's army who marches to the orders of an unseen force. What one notices upon first meeting Susie is her passion for the mission to which she has been called. Whatever path your conversation may take, it is only a matter of time before she is talking about the same people whom Jesus Himself proclaimed He came into the world to save the poor, the brokenhearted, the captive, and the bruised.

Susie's personal journey to become so unconditionally obedient to the call of God was not easy. Her obedience to God's call required that she give up a career in nursing, a more "comfortable" path in which she could have focused more on herself and her own needs, and a more leisurely paced life with much more "down" time. But God came with special orders, and she answered the clarion call with radical, unconditional obedience.

31 Days of Mountaintop Miracles is her incredible story as seen through the eyes of a heart focused on looking at life as the miracle it is. It is a collection of stories of what God will do when someone has the audacity to believe, and not just to hear but to obey His voice. I have been staggered by watching what God has done and continues to do in Susie Jennings' life. I think you will be, too.

Enjoy!

—DAN DEAN, LEAD SINGER, *PHILLIPS, CRAIG & DEAN* AND SENIOR PASTOR, HEARTLAND CHURCH, CARROLLTON, TEXAS

*He will swallow up death forever. The Sovereign
LORD will wipe away the tears from all faces; he
will remove his people's disgrace from all the earth.
The LORD has spoken.*
Isaiah 25:8 (NIV)

INTRODUCTION
A JOURNEY OF THE HEART

It was Tuesday, March 9, 1993, a beautiful spring-like day in Dallas. Flowers had started to bloom, the trees were filling out, and the scent of fresh life was in the air. Although the season was light with promise, my heart was heavy with concern. My beloved husband of nine years, David, had left our home earlier that day under a cloud of manic despondency and had not returned. David suffered from a chemical imbalance called "Serotonin Deficiency," which caused him to be severely depressed. His depression worsened when he lost a close family member, then his job, and again when his psychiatrist moved to another state. His agitation, paranoia, and manic episodes grew. I was a Registered Nurse and worked as a supervisor in the recovery room of a major medical center—yet no matter how I tried to help, there was nothing I could do to reach him.

On the day of his disappearance, he threatened that he was going to leave and go live in a place where no one knew him. He said he wanted to start a new life. I did what I could to get him to stay—I even called his parents to come over, but David had already left the house when they arrived. A sales receipt showed that he filled his car with gas that afternoon. Because of all the extenuating circumstances leading up to his disappearance, including his diminished mental and emotional capacity, I was able to immediately file a formal report with the Mesquite Police Department. On the evening of that beautiful spring day in March, David officially became a missing person nationwide.

A Worried Heart

It's been many years, but I remember it like yesterday. The difficult days that followed left an indelible imprint on my heart. The first night he was gone, I paced the floor and repeatedly looked out the front and back windows, praying that I would see him return. I finally went to bed, but sleep evaded me. I sang hymns and read a story about a woman who had lost her daughter. I found comfort only in the Lord and in His promises, but most of all in prayer and from Scriptures. That night the Lord led me to this verse in 2 Timothy 1:7, "For God has not given us the spirit of fear, but of power and of love and of a sound mind" (NIV). It brought me comfort to know that if I was obedient and trusted His Word, the Lord would take away my fears, anxieties, and uncertainties. Over the next few days I grew increasingly concerned, yet I remained hopeful. I went to work, and each evening when I returned home I would pray that David's white car would be parked in the garage and that he would be waiting for me. Yet there was no David, only an empty house and a deep sense of loneliness and growing apprehension.

David was missing four days when my mom came to Dallas to be with me. It was no accident she had arrived in California from the Philippines just a few days before David disappeared. I praise the Lord for bringing my precious mother to me at a time when I needed her so desperately. It was a bittersweet reunion. I was so grateful to see her but saddened that David was not with me to welcome her. That day, the Lord gave me verse five from Psalm 30 to claim as my own: "For His anger is but for a moment. His favor is for life; weeping may endure for a night, but joy comes in the morning." This Scripture gave me hope because it made me think that David was alive and probably trying to find a job somewhere. Eventually, there would once again be joy in our home. Every night my mother and I knelt down and prayed together, hoping.

A Hopeful Heart

The second week, the Lord gave me another hopeful verse, "I will preserve his life, I will keep him alive and he will be blessed upon the earth, and he will not be given to the will of his enemies." This verse from Psalm 41:2 gave me hope that David was surely alive.

"Look at this verse, Mother." I pointed to the page as we sat together reading our Bibles. "It says, 'I will keep him alive!'" My mother's smile encouraged me. God is so kind. He gave me hope to keep me functioning.

On the third week, the Lord gave me Psalm 116:15, "Precious in the sight of the Lord is the death of His saints." When I read this verse, I thought the message was just an accidental coincidence because I had been reading the Psalms chapter by chapter since David's disappearance. I did not like this particular verse, so I closed my Bible and reached for my hymnal. "Lord, give me a joyful and reassuring hymn," I said aloud as I randomly opened the hymnal. The Lord took me to the hymn, "It Is Well with My Soul." It says, "When sorrows like sea billows roll . . . " I did not think that was the right song, so I turned to another random page where He gave me this song, "He Hideth My Soul." When I came to the last stanza I sang, "When clothed in His brightness transported I rise to meet Him in clouds of the sky..."

Suddenly, it became clear. *Lord, none of this is a coincidence, is it? You are talking to me about death.* The next day, I opened my Bible, hoping I would come upon a verse that would assure me that David was still alive. Within moments, my eyes once again fell on these words from Psalm 116:15, "Precious in the sight of the Lord is the death of His saints."

The Heart Knows

In my heart, I knew God was telling me that David was gone, but another part of me did not want to believe it. I had never felt so near to the Lord as during those agonizing days. He was my rock. My mother and I both prayed earnestly and almost without ceasing. I was so thankful she was with me—until the day her prayer focus shifted.

"Dear Jesus, please send us someone who will lead us to David's body."

At first I was upset. *How could she say that? Why would she voice such a prayer?*

But in His wisdom and divine grace, the Lord was actually using my mother to prepare me for the truth. Today, I'm thankful she was obedient in praying aloud what the Lord had placed so strongly on her heart. One day, an unexpected visitor knocked on my front door. It was Wednesday, April 7, almost one month from the day David went missing. It was the officer assigned to David's case, Detective Bradshaw.

"Mrs. Jennings, your husband's car was found in Atoka, Oklahoma, on March 13. I just found the report today."

"March 13?" I shouted. "March 13? That was weeks ago!"

"I know, Mrs. Jennings, and I'm very sorry. The report from the Atoka Sheriff's office was buried under a mountain of paperwork. I came here as soon as I found it." He held a copy of the report, and I could hear my mother praying in the background as I started to ask the obvious question.

"Was his body …"

"No one was in the car. It was listed only as an abandoned vehicle and was towed to the impound lot where it's been sitting ever since."

At first I was so angry. My initial thought was to sue the local police department, but immediately the Holy Spirit reminded me that God was still in control. Everything that was happening was happening for a reason. I began to feel a small ray of hope that perhaps all was not lost after all.

"Did the police check with people to see if anyone saw him?" I asked. "Where was his car abandoned? Are they sure it was abandoned? Maybe he was at a job or in a store or visiting someone. What if they left him stranded without a vehicle, and he doesn't know how to get his car back? What if he's been homeless since they took it? We need to go up there …" I was ready to grab my purse and head out the door that very minute when the detective reached for my arm.

"Mrs. Jennings, David's car was found in a very secluded field, far from any homes or businesses. I'm going up there first thing in the morning with a team of officers to look for his …to look around." It was clear by his pained expression that the detective was deeply grieved by the situation.

I reached out and put my hand gently on his arm.

"I'm going with you," I said.

He started to object but quickly realized that would be futile.

It seems strange to say this now, but at that moment peace enveloped my heart. God had prepared me for this, and I desired to place everything into His hands and trust His will.

A Heavy Heart

That next morning, on Thursday, April 8, I got out of bed with a profound heaviness in my heart. Pastors Luis Pantoja, Tom Roxas and Mark Santos, my father-in-law, Charles Jennings, Detective Bradshaw, and I drove to Atoka, Oklahoma, to look for David. A part of me was still hopeful, but there was also a part of me that knew something was terribly wrong. The sheriff and four deputies went with us to the secluded area where David's car was found. I looked out over the vast acreage as we split up into groups to comb the field. My prayers that day were very specific.

Lord, I have two requests. If my David is in heaven with You, please let us find his earthly body today, and if he is out here—let me be the one to find him.

The Lord's ways are higher than our ways, and He answered my prayers in His own way.

While we searched, a single gunshot rang out from a deputy's gun as a signal. I stopped in my tracks and looked up to see everyone rushing toward the deputy as he shouted.

"I found a body and I think it's him."

At last the search was over—in an instant the gnawing pain of the unknown became the heart-wrenching pain of reality. The Lord graciously kept me from discovering David first. Because of the cooler spring weather, much of David's body was preserved, but thirty days under the elements of sunshine and rain had left him in bad shape— parts of his body were badly decomposed. It was a shock to discover that my husband had killed himself with a gun.

My legs went limp. I lost all my strength and fell to the ground. I did not ask the Lord why this had happened because I knew He was in control. However, the anger I felt toward David consumed me. We promised to grow old together. Now he had left me all alone.

"Why? David, why?" I cried out.

Pastor Luis helped me to my feet. I was numb, my body was in shock. I pulled away and cried at the top of my lungs, wanting God to hear me.

"God, give me strength. God, give me strength!" I screamed.

I immediately felt a bolt, like electricity, come from my feet, travel up my legs, and then shoot out of my mouth. I felt an immediate peace as my heavy burden of sorrow fell away. I walked out of that field of despair as if my feet were not touching the ground, with an indescribable peace that could only have come from God.

We buried David the day before Easter Sunday. He was supposed to sing at church on Easter, but instead of singing the song "Heaven," he was already in heaven singing his song before the Lord.

Now, the Lord is my husband as Isaiah 54:5 says, "The Lord, your Maker will be your husband."

A Heart that Is Called

Five months later, my next-door neighbor took his own life in his backyard. I was baking a cake in my kitchen when he pulled the trigger on the other side of our adjacent fence. The Lord was so gracious in shielding me from either seeing him or hearing the gunshot. When I learned of this desperate act I asked the Lord, "Why? Why are people so hopeless?"

He answered by giving me a vision through a dream. In my dream, I was knocking at people's doors, sharing the gospel. *People are hopeless, Susie, because they don't know my Son. I want you to go where they live and show them who He is.*

God wanted me to share Jesus' love with people who have no hope. I could do that! At the time I felt I was being called to minister to widows like myself, and to single mothers. Out of my sorrow and pain, I organized "The Lord's Bride Fellowship." But I soon came to learn that wasn't God's only plan for me. I began to feel in my spirit that God wanted me to do more—but I didn't know what that "more" was. And so I began to ask Him.

"God, what can I do for You *and* the community?"

One Sunday in October 1993, He showed me. I had just finished teaching a preschool class in Sunday school and I was driving in downtown Dallas when I heard a voice so loud it startled me.

Look to your left, Susie. Now.

I was driving by the Canton Street Bridge and as I looked to my left I saw more than a hundred homeless men and women living in cardboard box "homes" with trash bags as their windows. I slowed my car to a crawl as I stared. I had driven in this area for ten years, but I did not care to notice them. Then I heard the same booming voice again.

"You go under that bridge in person!"

I was shocked not only by the voice, but by my vehement response to it as well.

"No! Not me! Those people are violent and crazy. They are bums, and they might hurt me!"

Then I heard God's voice again; this time it was gentle and loving.

"Susie, it was you who asked Me, 'What can I do for You and the community?' This is what you can do."

I couldn't imagine working with homeless people in any capacity.

The Heart of a Child

As a young girl growing up in the Philippines, I watched my mother exhibit a saint-like quality in ministering to the homeless. We didn't have a lot, but we had enough to share. People would come to our home at all hours begging for food. They were often dirty and unkempt, and I did not like it at all when they ate in our kitchen, at our table! I felt like they were eating my food and occupying my space!

I was an obedient child, and I loved my mother, so I did what she asked to help, but I'm sorry to say that my spirit was far from willing. There were times when my displeasure with the entire situation was clearly obvious, when my pride and arrogance got in the way. But instead of scolding me, my kind mother would impart words of wisdom.

"We are not rich in money, Susie, but we are rich in God's love and blessings."

As if sharing our food wasn't enough, my Mom would sometimes give these people small chores like chopping wood to be used for cooking.

"It is important for everyone to feel useful, Susie, to know they are contributing."

Well, I was contributing, and I didn't like it one bit.

My feelings of dislike and fear of the homeless grew when I was at the marketplace one day doing a chore for my mom and without provocation, a homeless lady came up to me and slapped me across the face. I had never spoken to her before, although I knew that she and her husband and daughter would often come to our house and beg. The unprovoked violence shocked me.

Who in their right mind would do such a thing?

Sadly, this woman wasn't in her "right mind." I was too

young to understand the serious mental and emotional disability issues many homeless people struggle with every day. As a young girl, there was so much about this needy population that I didn't understand.

And frankly, I didn't want to understand it. All I knew growing up was that I could not stand homeless people. Period.

In essence, I grew up with this disenfranchised population. Yet when I became an adult, graduated from nursing school, and moved to the United States, their needs were the furthest thing from my mind. I loved the Lord and longed to do His will. I developed a strong work ethic and a generous volunteer spirit. But doing anything in, around, or for the homeless? No way. Not in this lifetime. However, God in His infinite wisdom had other plans.

AN AWAKENED HEART

All I could think about as I drove by that bridge and saw the city of cardboard, was my mother's example of gracious humility and care for the homeless. She had planted a seed of deep compassion in my heart that I had done nothing to nurture over the years. Clearly, it was time for my apathy to end. It was time to get rid of the pride and arrogance I felt toward these people—people who God loved just as much as He loved me.

Suddenly, the Holy Spirit convicted me. Had anyone helped David when he was alone and afraid? In a way, his car had become his cardboard box in the last days of his life. How many of these homeless men and women suffered from the debilitating effects of mental illness as David had? How many are fighting a desperate battle with the demon of depression? How many are feeling hopeless?

"Forgive me, God. What can I give to these needy people?" I said aloud.

"Blankets!" God's one word reply was clear.

It was warm when David went missing in the spring. But now it was late fall, and contrary to what some may think, it can get very cold in the evening in Dallas, Texas. My heart began to break for these precious souls huddled together under cardboard boxes with little else to protect them.

In the time it took to drive from one end of the bridge to the other, the Lord took away my decades-old fear and loathing of this needy population and changed my hardened heart towards the homeless. This is what my dream meant by "go to where they live and show them who Jesus is." The next day, I went to work at the hospital with a plan.

"I'm collecting money for blankets for the homeless," I said to anyone who crossed my path. "Anything you can give will help." I boldly held my hands out as doctors and nurses emptied their pockets, wallets, and purses of cash, and wrote checks.

Volunteers from the Filipino American Baptist Church, a mission church of First Baptist Dallas, went with me under that bridge in November, the Sunday before Thanksgiving. We distributed 100 blankets and did one-on-one evangelism together. Many homeless people found hope in Jesus.

The next month we returned, the Sunday before Christmas. This time, we brought an evangelist with us who preached on top of a pickup truck. More people accepted Jesus as Lord. We named the fledgling project "Operation Care." Romans 8:28 was the verse I claimed: "And we know that God causes all things to work together for good to those who love God, to those who are called according to His purpose" (Psalm 56:8). Yes, there is great suffering in this world. However, there is also great compassion, love, and hope. God feels our pain, shares our sorrow, and places our tears in His bottle.

Charles Spurgeon said, "A tried Christian, afterwards … grows rich by his losses, he rises by his falls, he lives by dying, and becomes full by being emptied." Although Satan meant David's death for evil, the Lord eventually used it for good.

A Heart for Miracles

Without exception, each step I walk on this journey of life has been a growing experience that strengthens me and teaches me the powerful role of prayer and unconditional obedience in my daily walk with my beloved Savior. It was through the deep pain of loss that I was able to find uplifting J-O-Y that is ours when we focus on *Jesus*, *Others* and then *Yourself*. It is this kind of joy that has opened the eyes of my heart to see the miracles that God provides every day.

It is this never-ending supply of miracles woven together layer upon layer that makes up the intricate and colorful fabric of Operation Care International. Please allow me to share the legacy of a community blanket distribution project that through God's grace and guidance has grown into a worldwide outreach ministry where we have reached nearly 24,000 children in nine countries and over 130,000 homeless men, women and children in the Dallas Metroplex area.

Today, I invite you to walk with our Lord and me for *31 Days of Mountaintop Miracles.*

And at the end of each day, I challenge you to "Master a Miracle Mindset" as you train yourself to look closely at the blessings of your life through the eyes of the God who deeply loves you—the God who has a miraculous plan and purpose for your life.

It is written in 1 John 4:19, "We love because He first loved us." I praise God for my mother who is now in heaven and for her heart of love and compassion towards the poor. Now I am serving the homeless, people I did not like, in a ministry I did not want. At the end of the day, I am my mother's daughter. And it all started in her tiny kitchen.

Where did your miracles start? And where are they going to take you today? May God bless and keep you on the journey!

In His service until He comes,

Susie

Part One

MIRACLES OF GOD'S PROMISES AND PLANS

It all began with one blanket . . .

and has grown beyond thousands of blankets! Praise God!

DAY 1

It All Started with Blankets

*Trust God from the bottom of your heart; don't try to
figure out everything on your own. Listen for God's
voice in everything you do, everywhere you go;
He's the one who will keep you on track.*
Proverbs 3:5-6 (MSG)

Since 1993, I have been giving away blankets to the homeless in the streets of Dallas. This outreach was a labor of love and obedience that I felt called by God to do. Family, friends, and co-workers contributed the money that enabled me to purchase the blankets. Virtually every Saturday, my mother and I would go shopping. As soon as the trunk was full we would go home, unload the blankets, stack them in the garage, and leave to buy more. My loving mother was in her 80s, but no one could push a cart loaded with blankets like she could!

Mom always had a heart for those in need. When I was a child in the Philippines, she would feed the hungry homeless in our tiny kitchen. It was a blessing that she had come to live with me after my husband David died and that she so graciously helped with this blanket distribution project. One especially cold season, we went to five different suburbs to buy blankets. We also taped a "Four Spiritual Laws" Gospel tract to each blanket and prayed over them. The entire project was quite a process, but one that we both did with unconditional obedience because we knew this outreach was God's plan.

I would always carry a supply of these blankets in the trunk of my car. Every time I would see a homeless person, I would stop my car, open the trunk and give that person in need a blanket—and a hopeful word from the Lord.

By the fall of 2001, I had about 500 blankets in my garage. They were stacked so high that every time we opened the car doors, blankets would fall upon our heads. I was beginning to feel bad for dragging my Mom with me every Saturday to buy blankets. Truthfully, I was getting weary myself, and I wished someone would help us. In addition to this ministry, I worked a full-time job as a nurse supervisor in the Recovery Room at Baylor University Medical Center.

I knew this ministry to the homeless was God's plan for my life—and for the community. When He convicted me to carry out this mission, I wasn't sure where it would go—only that I needed to trust in Him for guidance. My responsibility was to pray, listen and offer unconditional obedience. One day, I heard God's still small voice within my heart.

It is time to become a nonprofit organization.

How can I do that? I responded in my spirit. *I'm not a businesswoman. I can't even balance my checkbook, David used to do that.*

The following week, my good friend Nena Schnitman called.

"Susie, I've been thinking about something. Why don't you become a nonprofit? You've been at this for what—almost eight years? It's time to take this volunteer project of yours to the next level. Nate knows all the legal stuff about setting up a nonprofit organization. He can help you."

Nate was Nena's husband. Clearly, this was another facet of God's bigger plan, and I thanked Him for opening the doors to a solution so quickly. I went to their home, and Nate helped me complete all the paperwork to apply for nonprofit status, and thus Operation Care Dallas was "officially" born. Our first three board members were Nena, another friend named Manel Diwa, and myself. My mother and I were no longer alone on the journey. Now, we had a real Board of Directors. The fact that the three of us barely had a clue what we were doing didn't seem to bother us. We knew the most important thing—that we were walking in the midst of a miraculous plan, and as long as we remained willing to listen and obey unconditionally, God would take care of the rest.

When God gives the vision, He gives the provision.

MASTERING A MIRACLE MINDSET

1. What is the "blanket" that God can use to start your journey into a miracle?
2. Is there something you feel God wants you to do today, big or small, to fulfill a special purpose?
3. If so, are you ready to listen to His voice and obey this command so God can take you to the "next level"?

WHAT IS YOUR MIRACLE MINDSET FOR TODAY?

_____

_____

_____

Ron Hall, Lexon Cole, Susie and
Denver Moore at our first gala.

DAY 2

A Less-Than-a-Minute Miracle

*If you need wisdom if you want to know what God
wants you to do—ask Him, and He will gladly tell you.
He will not resent your asking.*
James 1:5 (NLT)

One of the delights of my life is spending time with the Lord. Early one Monday morning, I was kneeling at the foot of my bed, praying and asking God to show me His will regarding the location of where we should hold our upcoming special event. This was no ordinary event. It would be our first major fundraising gala for Operation Care Dallas.

I started the ministry in 1993 to distribute blankets to the homeless in the Dallas Metroplex area with a few dedicated volunteers. In 2001 we officially became Operation Care Dallas and within a few years, Operation Care International would grow into a worldwide outreach.

My prayers that summer morning in 2008 were intentional and specific.

Lord, I need to hear your voice.

I was dealing with a sensitive situation, as the Board of Directors was divided regarding the venue for the fundraiser. It was understandable that for economic reasons, the chairman of the board wanted to hold our event in a local church. However, since this was our first significant fundraiser and would therefore set precedence, I felt it should be independent of any particular church, and several board members agreed. As an interdenominational nonprofit organization, Operation Care Dallas provided services to the homeless, no matter the individual's race, creed, color, or ethnic origin. I felt it was important that there was no question whether we were under the umbrella of any specific church or denomination.

As we debated about which avenue to take, my responsibility had been to research local hotels and put together some numbers. The evening before, the Lord placed it in my heart that our event should be at a specific hotel whose name kept coming to the top of my list during my research. And so, during my prayer time that morning, I asked God for a very clear sign. I did not doubt that God would answer my prayer His way, but I wanted a clear answer because we needed to decide soon.

While intently deep in prayer, the phone rang. Normally, I would let it roll over into voice mail and return the call later, but there was an urging in my spirit to answer the call immediately. So, I said a quick "amen," got up from kneeling, sat on the right side of the bed and answered the phone on the nightstand.

When I said, "hello," the voice on the other end of the line was my answer from God. "Hello, Susie, this is Linda from the Intercontinental Hotel in Dallas. I just want to follow up about the possibility of having your event in our hotel. We would certainly love to do everything we can to help make that possible." I immediately slid from my perch on the side of the bed back down to the floor where I knelt in my prayer position as we continued this divinely inspired phone conversation—a true miracle in the making—because the Intercontinental Hotel was the exact location the Lord had placed on my heart the night before.

When I hung up the phone, I shook my head in amazement and praised the Holy Name of Jesus. Once again I was assured that God had a definite plan for this ministry.

"Thank you, Lord! That was one of the fastest answers to prayer I've ever experienced!"

Less than one minute from asking for a sign—just a few seconds in fact! That was good enough confirmation for me. I went to the Board of Directors shortly thereafter and shared God's clear answer to my prayer—to all of our prayers. Further confirmation came when the church being considered suddenly called to inform us that a scheduling conflict would preclude them from being able to host the event, and this was final assurance to all that God had indeed spoken.

The inaugural Operation Care Dallas gala fundraiser was held at the Intercontinental Hotel in Dallas in October 2008. Since then, the spectacular annual event has become one of the highlights in the lives of our dedicated sponsors and donors. It is a joy-filled event as together we celebrate what happens when we focus on J-O-Y in the form of focusing on Jesus-Others-Yourself.

There is true joy in prayer . . . and after all, isn't true joy what we are all praying for?

MASTERING A MIRACLE MINDSET

How can spending time with the Lord every day help you see life experiences in a more miraculous way?

Gala event, Dallas, TX.

DAY 3

A Leader Who Caught the Vision

*God can do anything you know—far more than you
could ever imagine or guess or request in your wildest
dreams! He does it not by pushing us around but by
working within us, His Spirit deeply and gently within us.*
Ephesians 3:20 (MSG)

In August of 2004, I attended a Marketplace Ministries gala at the Hilton Anatole Hotel in Dallas where a well-respected husband-and-wife team were honored for their years of ministry to help families thrive. After the event, guests had the opportunity to wait in line and personally meet these godly servants. These brief one-on-one greetings would take place on the stage as guests were able to talk briefly with one of the honorees. I had a prompting in my heart to talk to the woman and ask her to pray for the newest vision that God had placed in my heart.

My friend Sam and I waited patiently in line, and when it was my turn to speak, I asked this renowned Christian leader to pray for me. I told her about the Operation Care ministry and shared the vision for our first annual Christmas event. I did not want to jeopardize her gracious hospitality, so I'm afraid I rushed my explanation, but it went something like this.

"Operation Care ministers to thousands of homeless people in the Dallas Metroplex area. This year we will have our first-ever Christmas party to celebrate Jesus' birthday, and the homeless will be the guests. We are having the event at the Dallas Convention Center, and the heart of the event is prayer and evangelism. The trademark will be foot washing. We will have hundreds of volunteers to help us at foot-washing stations, and give haircuts and make-overs. We will distribute clothing, socks, and shoes. We are going to have medical assessments with flu shots and blood pressure with blood sugar checks for the adults. The children will receive socks, shoes, and toys. We're going to have lots of food and refreshments, and we will even have entertainment and a choir!"

When I was done with my excited and animated presentation, she shook her head in amazement and assured me she would pray. I had no doubt this awesome woman of God would keep her word and it felt good to know that such a powerful prayer warrior would issue a word on our behalf to God the Father. When I walked off the stage, I felt an unusual combination of energetic calm—energized at having had the opportunity to speak with this respected Christian leader, and that peace that passes all understanding when you know God is in control. When I reached the floor level, I heard this fellow prayer warrior calling to me. My friend Sam was still on the stage. She turned to him and said, "Tell Susie that her vision is small!" Then she looked at me and said, "Pray that this vision will go worldwide!"

I will always remember those words. They encouraged my heart greatly then and continue to do so years later. I admired this esteemed woman greatly, and I believe it was God who placed that prompting in her heart to call out and tell me to pray for a worldwide vision, and I took her advice seriously. Her words of encouragement echo one of my favorite quotes from Dr. Norman Vincent Peale: "Pray big. Think big. Believe big." Since that day when this Christian leader caught the Operation Care vision and advised me to think bigger, we have been to nine countries! We have reached nearly 24,000 homeless and impoverished children in the Philippines, India, Africa, Taiwan, China, Indonesia, Cambodia, Jordan, and Israel. We have connected these precious souls to Christian churches and organizations and have built schools and even a medical clinic where children can become physically and spiritually healthy as they receive the hopeful and healing Word of God.

God in His infinite wisdom and grace has made it possible for me to meet additional Christian leaders who have spoken words of prayer and prophecy into my life and into the Operation Care ministry, leaders like Dan Dean, Senior Pastor of the Heartland Church, who has graciously written the foreword to this book. I enjoy the music of Phillips, Craig & Dean and to know that their Lead Singer, this respected man of God, believes in what we are doing and prays for us, is yet another miracle in a long and growing list. Indeed, God is working miracles as Operation Care International continues to expand worldwide, and more people continue to catch the vision!

MASTERING A MIRACLE MINDSET

1. Are there Christian leaders—contemporary heroes of the faith—whose lives and examples you look up to?
2. Do you seek the wise advice and encouragement of such "tried and tested" ministers and leaders?

Operation Care Philippines our first international event.

*As a result of our efforts, two boys were
able to undergo cleft palate surgery.*

DAY 4

Operation Care Dallas Goes International

I will bless her with abundant provisions;
her poor I will satisfy with food.
Psalm 132:15 (NIV)

I was thoroughly excited to be going back to the Philippines in July for my nursing class reunion. My initial plan was to spend some time with friends and family and relax a bit before my return to the States. However, God had other plans.

In January, I began to have faint thoughts and visions about conducting some type of outreach to the homeless population while I was there, perhaps something informal at one of the local churches. But at 6:00 AM on January 31, 2008, I awoke to a clear and concise prompting from the Lord that He had something far bigger in mind. No more vague thoughts or visions; this message from the Lord was crystal clear: Operation Care Philippines was going to help homeless children in Iloilo City on Panay Island in the Philippines.

Gulp.

We had never done an international event, but I knew I heard His voice loud and clear in my spirit.

Okay, Lord. This is only six months away, and I don't

know anyone who can lead the team and organize things in the Philippines. So, I'm really going to need you to point me in the right direction—soon!

The day after God spoke to me; I called up Kelly Savage of Soles for Kidz. I shared the vision God gave me. "Can you donate 500 pairs of shoes?" I asked.

"I can do better," she responded. "I'll give you double that number!"

Thank you, Jesus! This was an immediate confirmation that Operation Care Philippines was truly from God. I contacted the Board of Directors; they all voted and gave their complete support to do the project.

Next, I called Buckner International. They would give over a thousand pairs of shoes. By three months before the scheduled event, we were able to gather 2,800 pairs of shoes. As word spread and churches and supporters heard of the mission, they gave us personal-care products to distribute. Everything was coming together in a miraculous way!

I contacted my cousin, Mercy Bedona, who was also a Registered Nurse and the head of the Human Resources Department of the Central Philippine University in Iloilo City. This is the Christian university where I graduated from nursing in 1978. Mercy ended up organizing the whole event, with thirteen churches and three large organizations that joined forces to help make our first international project, Operation Care Philippines, a huge success.

Our theme was "Changing Lives, Changing the World," and we did just that as about 1,704 children responded to the gospel presentation. And because of God's provision, we distributed 2,000 backpacks, Bibles, T-shirts, socks, shoes, personal-care products, and toys.

Oh, and I also had a wonderful time at my class reunion! Even my classmates volunteered during the event. Their lives were changed as well. A life-changing experience—Yes, God is so good. His goodness transcends all boundaries, not only the boundaries of nations, but even of life and death. A few years later, Mercy was taken by God to His heavenly dwelling. One day, all His children will have a reunion there, and that will be a miracle to last for all eternity.

Mastering a Miracle Mindset

1. When God gives you a project, do you know who to call for support? God often uses people to carry His message or clarify His vision.
2. Are you able to make wise use of the "connections" that God has provided? Networking is very practical.
3. Do you courageously ask for assistance? Remember, the Word of God says "Ask and it shall be given you."

What is your miracle mindset for today?

_____

_____

_____

Mrs. Dottie Thompson obeyed God unconditionally and planted the seed for this ministry to grow.

DAY 5

LORD, YOUR NAME IS AT STAKE!

Do not be anxious about anything, but in every situation, by prayer and petition, with thanksgiving, present your requests to God. And the peace of God, which transcends all understanding, will guard your hearts and your minds in Christ Jesus.
PHILIPPIANS 4:6-7 (NIV)

It would be our first holiday event, and Operation Care Christmas Gift 2004 was already heralded as "The City's Largest Christmas Party for the Homeless." The vision to give a birthday party for Jesus where the guests of honor are the outcasts of society, our homeless population, was something I shared with our Operation Care Chairman of the Board, Ron Batts. We both felt the Lord telling us that this particular community outreach was going to have long term—and far-reaching success. The theme of the party was "Reuniting the Family, A Christmas to Remember!" Our plan was to allow the homeless to use our phones in November to call their families ahead of time and invite them to come to the Dallas Convention Center for a family reunion. Many people who find themselves homeless have become estranged and separated from their families, and this would be a perfect opportunity for God to heal hearts and repair relationships.

The budget for this event was mind-boggling—it would take $100,000 to provide Bibles, shoes, socks, sleeping bags, blankets, food, entertainment, medical screenings, and personal-care products. We would even have a makeover area, with skilled volunteers to give haircuts and facials.

The heart of our ministry is prayer and evangelism, and the trademark act is foot washing, which we planned to do at the party. A symbol of humility and service just like Jesus' own example, we knew from experience that this act would open the doors for unexpected miracles to happen in the hearts and souls of everyone participating—for both giver and receiver.

The number of homeless in and around the Dallas Metroplex areas are beyond comprehension for most people. We were expecting 6,000 to 7,000 homeless men, women, and indigent kids. The only place we could conduct an operation of this magnitude was the Dallas Convention Center—a facility of over 100,000 square feet!

We had literally over a thousand volunteers, and everything was coming together—except our funds. Our event was thirty days away, and we had only twenty dollars that was given to us by an eight-year-old boy from Cleveland, Ohio. Young Nick broke his piggy bank and gave all his money to his mom, Alice, to give to Operation Care. In giving all he had for the sake of helping the homeless, Nick reminded me of the boy in the Bible who gave everything he had to Jesus: two fish and five loaves, which the Lord Jesus Christ multiplied to feed a crowd of 5,000 people. A true miracle if ever there was one!

Lord, please multiply our twenty dollars!

Praying for funding miracles isn't unusual in this ministry. It costs a lot to reach so many in need—yet God has always had His hand on this outreach. I trust Him to provide, I believe in His promises, and I know He has a plan!

However, this time when I was praying for a miracle, I heard myself say something unfamiliar. "Lord, please do something, because Your Name is at stake!"

I knew within my heart that I was called to help the homeless and to help give them this Christmas party. I did have faith that God would provide, but I won't lie; I was starting to feel desperate and knew that God was our only answer.

That same night, I got a call from Dianne Etheredge, the chairman of our fund-raising committee. There was excitement in her voice.

"Are you sitting down?" Dianne asked me. I wasn't, but I proceeded to sit down.

"I am now. What's up?"

"I went to see a good friend, Dottie Thompson this morning; she got out of the hospital two weeks ago, but this was the soonest she felt up to having visitors. She told me that before she got sick, she had planned to give a donation to charity but was not able to do it. You'll never guess what she asked me."

"What? What did she ask?" I was sure I was turning blue from holding my breath.

"She asked how much it would take to have the Christmas party at the Dallas Convention Center, and when I told her $100,000, she practically jumped for joy! Susie, that was the exact amount the Lord placed on her heart to give away! She wanted to donate it to charity before she went into the hospital but wasn't able to. She's going to have a check for us tomorrow!"

Praise God!

I figured out the timing and realized that God answered my specific prayer in about the span of one working day. I pleaded for help at ten o'clock that morning, and ten hours later God answered that prayer. I learned that when we ask God in specifics, reminding Him that His Name is at stake, and always walking in obedience, He will often answer far more abundantly than we ever dreamed. Once again, God resolved our financial need, and once again proved that when God gives the vision He will also give the provision!

The party on December 18, 2004, was a huge success with almost 10,000 in attendance. It was the beginning of a landmark tradition, our annual Nation's Largest Christmas Party for the homeless. Because an eight-year-old boy believed and gave all he had, the Lord multiplied his donation by providing through the kindness and generosity of Mrs. Dottie Thompson who just got out of the hospital and who obeyed God unconditionally. I am forever grateful to the Lord for blessing us with these gestures of kindness from people whose big hearts gave so much joy to thousands of lives. They are pure examples of how we show our love for God when we share our love with others.

More than a few miracles played out during that Christmas season and again at the party, as many families were reunited, volunteers were changed, and hearts were softened by this truly humbling experience. After all, if Jesus was present in the flesh at His own birthday celebration, who do you think He would choose to celebrate with—the kings or the outcasts? No question about it, He would be with the outcasts and the downtrodden, and no question about it, He was present at our party that day—just ask anyone who was there.

Today, many people are aware of the annual events that have become Operation Care traditions. Yet these hallmark events were all born from answered prayer and come to fruition every year the same way, as literally thousands of people listen to God and offer unconditional obedience in carrying out His plans.

When he had finished washing their feet, he put on his clothes and returned to his place. "Do you understand what I have done for you?" he asked them. "You call me 'Teacher' and 'Lord,' and rightly so, for that is what I am. Now that I, your Lord and Teacher, have washed your feet, you also should wash one another's feet. I have set you an example that you should do as I have done for you. Very truly I tell you, no servant is greater than his master, nor is a messenger greater than the one who sent him. Now that you know these things, you will be blessed if you do them. JOHN 13:12-17 (NIV)

MASTERING A MIRACLE MINDSET

1. Is there a "piggy bank" in your life that you can sacrifice today, that God can multiply into a great ministry?
2. Are you trusting God for something today, and yet find yourself anxious?
3. Do you believe in God's perfect timing?

WHAT IS YOUR MIRACLE MINDSET FOR TODAY?

_____

_____

_____

Look at what happened in 17 seconds!

DAY 6

The Seventeen Seconds Miracle

*And it shall come to pass that, before they call, I will
answer; and while they are yet speaking, I will hear.*
Isaiah 65:24 (ASV)

As the earthly founder of Operation Care, I operate
under the guidance and provision of a Heavenly Founder, followed by a well-respected and fiscally responsible
Board of Directors. My heart was heavy but still hopeful that spring day in 2008 as we faced another financial
hurdle in the growing ministry. We were still "officially"
Operation Care Dallas, but ministry doors had begun to
open in other countries and we were about to go on our
first trip abroad. Operation Care Philippines was going to
be our first international outreach, and it would benefit
a staggering 2,000 or more homeless and slum children.
However, we needed $10,000 right away to order sup-
plies, and that amount wasn't even counting the rest of
the expenses needed for the trip. I was considering asking
the Board of Directors for the funds. The $10,000 would
pay the deposit on an order of 2,000 backpacks, Bibles,
T-shirts, and personal-care products for the kids. As I
began to formulate how I would present my case to the
board, I heard an audible voice.

"I will take care of it!"

The voice was confident and sure. I know in my spirit; it was the Lord speaking.

I planned to call our contact in the Philippines later that day when I got home from work; I was anxious to talk to her about this situation. I worked the evening shift as a nurse supervisor in a large medical center in Dallas. My habit every night after coming home from work is to check and answer all email communications. The majority of the incoming Operation Care e-mail come directly to me, and the numbers were increasing daily. I had checked all new messages and responded as needed. It was about 1:50 AM when I called my cousin, Mercy, in the Philippines where it was 2:50 PM. Mercy was the Human Resources Director of the Central Philippine University and also a Registered Nurse. She was in charge of the Operation Care Philippines project.

Mercy Yanson Bedona was herself a miracle! With a strong faith in God and a drastic change in her lifestyle, she was healed from Stage II cancer with no medication, chemotherapy, or radiation. She was eating right, getting enough rest, and exercising. It was always a joy to talk with her. When we were connected, I told Mercy about my dilemma.

"I want to ask the Operation Care board for $10,000, but I heard God's voice telling me He would take care of it."

"Did you really hear the voice of God?" She laughed.

"Yes, I heard it loud and clear!"

At that moment, I felt the immediate need to pray.

"Let's pray, now!" I started without hesitation and first thanked God for healing Mercy completely. Then, I asked Him to please provide the $10,000—in His own time. After I said, "amen," we said good-bye. As soon as I hung up the phone I heard God's voice within my heart saying, "Open up your computer."

"Lord, I already checked my email, who in the world would contact me at two o'clock in the morning?"

But if there's one thing I've learned in my growing relationship with God, it's the critical need to obey the voice of the Spirit. So, I sat down at my desk and opened my computer. I went directly to my email account and scanned the long list of messages I had already read, and there in the middle of all the opened emails was one lone message in bold, indicating it had not been opened.

How did I miss that?

It was from the Treasurer of Operation Care. I opened it and saw it was sent the day before at 11:43 AM.

Dear Susie,

You were wondering about funds for Operation Care Philippines. Well, praise the Lord for His blessings as the Mildred Azpell Foundation has donated $10,000 toward this project of "Changing Lives, Changing the World." I will be depositing the check in the bank this afternoon. God is good ALL THE TIME."

Serving Him together,
Bro. Jim

I shouted with glee and thanksgiving and praised God for the almost immediate answer to prayer. I grabbed the phone with childlike joy and called Mercy again.

"What did we just pray for?" I asked.

"We prayed for $10,000 to come in His time."

"Well, His time was about seventeen seconds from

when we hung up!"

I excitedly shared the good news and together we prayed and praised God for the miraculous way He so often provides. The money we needed was already in the bank when we prayed the first time. God is true to His Word. When we are faithful and obedient, He will always take care of our needs.

MASTERING A MIRACLE MINDSET

1. Do you recognize the "miracles" that are represented by the people in your life? Think of someone whose life is a miracle.
2. Is there someone you can call today to let that person know that you appreciate him or her?
3. Are you trusting God to always be on time in providing for a need?

WHAT IS YOUR MIRACLE MINDSET FOR TODAY?

_____

_____

_____

Part Two

Miracles of Answered Prayers

*My priceless wedding ring transformed
into a beautiful pendant.*

DAY 7

THE WIDOW'S PENDANT

If you remain in me and my words remain in you,
ask whatever you wish, and it will be done for you.
JOHN 15:7 (NIV)

It was our second annual fundraising event for Operation Care Dallas, and my heart swelled as I looked around the room. This was the first auction we had ever conducted. The items we were offering were selling quite well, and I watched the growing excitement on the faces of hundreds of guests as bidding on an exquisite pendant increased. The resounding applause brought a wave of emotion to my heart as the auctioneer pointed toward a new friend to the ministry and shouted . . .

"Sold to the gentleman—for seven thousand dollars!"

Thank you, Jesus! I praised His name, knowing that the funds we raised this night would provide for the physical and spiritual needs of homeless men, women, and children within the Dallas area. All of the items featured in our auction were donated, including this glorious pendant, and generous friends and supporters of the ministry had abundantly opened their hearts and their wallets to make our annual event successful. The gentleman who purchased the one-of-a-kind pendant for his wife was new to our growing family of benefactors, and when the auction was over, I silently thanked God for him as I took a final look at the pendant he would be taking home with him that night. I had prayed that this very special necklace would go to just the right person, and I felt God was answering my prayer in this kind and gracious man.

It truly was an exceptional piece of jewelry. Weighing in at almost thirty-one carats, the center stone was a brilliant blue topaz. It had a cluster of seven equally brilliant diamonds mounted at the top in a rich gold setting which was suspended from a gold chain. It looked as though it could be in a museum. I ran my fingers over the cool surface of the stone, remembering the first time I had laid eyes on it—the first time I had touched it.

It was years ago in Davao City, in the Philippines.

"It's beautiful." I held the loose stone in my palm and felt compelled to buy it on the spot. I had no idea what I would do with it, only that I couldn't leave without it. In May of the following year, I went back to the Philippines to visit my dear mother who was living with my sister, Christie, and her family. It was there, surrounded by the love of family in the country of my birth that the Lord placed an idea in my heart, an idea that took hold of me and wouldn't let go until I saw it through to completion.

I will use the seven diamonds from my wedding ring to highlight the topaz stone and have the gold from the ring melted to use as a mount. I'm going to have a keepsake pendant designed that will forever remind me of David.

My wedding ring was the last piece of jewelry I owned that emotionally connected me with David, my beloved late husband. I knew it was time to say good-bye, but it would feel good that every time I wore this pendant, it would allow me to keep the memory of our time together close to my heart. An expert Filipino artisan craftsman interpreted and created my vision perfectly. I treasured the finished product and before leaving my homeland, I purchased an elegant turquoise-colored gown to complement the stunning pendant. The pairing of the two made quite a statement.

Now, years later, I looked down at the pendant that no longer belonged to me, and I was at peace. The memories seemed fresh as they kissed my heart with emotion, and the power of God's love embraced me as I recalled the spirit-filled conversation leading up to this moment.

Not long after returning to the States, I found myself standing in front of a mirror in my home admiring my beautiful gown and pendant when I heard the Holy Spirit speak to my heart.

Donate your pendant to the Operation Care auction.

"What? Surely, I'm hearing things . . . not my beautiful pendant."

Donate your pendant to the Operation Care auction.

"Are you sure, God? Look how beautifully it matches my dress."

Donate your pendant to the Operation Care auction.

God's command was loud and clear.

"Okay Lord, if this is what you want."

The initial hesitation I felt quickly disappeared, and I willingly and joyfully agreed, giving everything I had left with a very joyful heart—just like the story of the widow's mite in the Bible. She gave everything she had plus her heart. Serving my Lord with unconditional obedience was—is—my goal.

Now, the pendant I donated had raised seven thousand dollars! More important, it was bought by a new friend and supporter of the Operation Care family. Praise God!

I said good-bye to a precious piece of jewelry and hello to an even more precious new friend. I knew this was God's plan. After the auction event, this new friend and his wife invited me to lunch. Week after week we tried to set a time that worked for all of us, yet week after week our schedules conflicted. It wasn't until Thanksgiving Day that we could celebrate with his family at a friend's house. We all had a wonderful time of fun and fellowship. When it was time to go, he and his wife walked me to my car. As we passed his truck, they abruptly stopped.

"Wait, Susie. We have something for you."

He reached into his truck, pulled out a tote bag and handed it to me.

"What's this?" I hadn't anticipated a gift. Spending Thanksgiving with these wonderful people had been blessing enough.

"Open it." They smiled.

I pulled out the square wooden box that was nestled inside the tote bag and opened it.

"My pendant!" I shouted, as my heart skipped a beat and tears of happiness filled my eyes.

"I bought it for my wife, but she said it belongs to you!"

I embraced my brother and sister-in-Christ, thanking them and thanking Jesus.

I'm certain now that God didn't allow us to have lunch together sooner because He wanted me to remember that very special Thanksgiving Day and to know that His thoughts are higher than our thoughts; His ways are higher than our ways. He had this miracle in mind from the start! Just like the story about the widow who gave Elijah her flour in a jar and a little oil in a jug, God showed me that when we willingly obey and give with a joyful heart, He will always provide—sometimes in miraculous ways.

But the story doesn't end there.

As members of the ECFA, Operation Care takes great pride in being financially responsible, and when our Auditor recorded the seven thousand dollars as income received, he informed me that even though the pendant had later been gifted back to me, that I was still able to claim the seven thousand dollars as a personal donation on my tax return. And because of that, it appeared the IRS now owed me! Clearly, God is in control, and I praise Him for who He is—a loving God of miracles.

Mastering a Miracle Mindset

Sometimes we gain the ability to see a miracle only after we have lost something valuable to us. Have you lost or been forced to give up someone or something precious in your life? If so, has it been possible for you to see God's miraculous hand through the difficult time?

What is your miracle mindset for today?

_____

_____

_____

Baylor University Medical Center, Dallas, TX.

DAY 8

A Miracle in Three Seconds

Let us then approach God's throne of grace with confidence, so that we may receive mercy and find grace to help us in our time of need.
Hebrews 4:16 (NIV)

I was driving to work for my evening shift as a nurse supervisor at the Post Anesthesia Care Unit of Baylor University Medical Center in Dallas. It had already been a long day.

I was feeling despondent and sad, as one of my friends had disappointed me. He promised to help at the warehouse where we were packing goods to ship to the Philippines for our summer outreach, Operation Care Philippines. He did not show up, and when I called, he told me he was busy and something came up. I did my best to be gracious and understanding, but I'll admit it was hard. Yet I had to understand that just because I was juggling a demanding full-time job and the responsibilities of a rapidly growing ministry, it didn't mean I had a free reign to insist that others drop everything to help me. I was already feeling down because we didn't have the finances needed for our trip to the Philippines, and we were leaving in two months. I looked at the cases of supplies, and I was overwhelmed by the prospect of the task in front of me.

Do not worry, my daughter. I'm right here beside you.

"Thank you, Jesus!" My words echoed in the vast warehouse. I knew I wasn't alone. God was with me, as were two other volunteers who arrived, and together we would accomplish what needed to be done to help literally thousands of children who desperately needed help. In order to survive on the streets, the homeless kids in the Philippines, as well as those living in the slums, often beg. They are shoeless, dirty, thin, emaciated children. They live in cemeteries, near old railroad tracks, and alongside marketplaces. They start working at a very early age making a living as scavengers in the dumps, carrying battered pieces of luggage or tattered shopping bags, and collecting waste paper, bottles, and metals for recycling.

Besides the hardships that come from the lack of shelter, sanitation and nutrition, some of these kids are substance abusers. This is a form of escape for so many of these tired little souls—escape from poverty, homelessness, violence, and abuse at home or in the streets. These were the kids the supplies were going to—the kids we wanted to introduce to Jesus and connect to churches after our event in the Philippines. Operation Care adopted Proverbs 19:17 from its inception, "Whoever is kind to the poor lends to the LORD" (NIV). I could only imagine the lives that would change because of our obedience to His command to go and help "the least of these."

Although I funneled as much money as I could into Operation Care from my own job, we existed and continued to expand because of God's grace and the generous financial support of some amazing private donors. An earlier $10,000 donation from a foundation grant provided for the initial payment for the backpacks, Bibles, T-shirts, and personal-care products we ordered. Yet we still needed $25,000 to ship everything, pay off the balance of the ordered goods, get our team to the island, and take care of expenses for the ten-day trip.

We had approached two of our most faithful and generous donors, a husband and wife team, and asked them to pray about donating something to help us reach out to these Filipino children. We just had to do something to break this vicious cycle. I prayed almost every day with my assistant that this wonderful couple would feel led by the spirit to lend their financial support—in any amount. With God as my copilot that day, I worked in the warehouse alongside our volunteers as we filled large boxes of shoes, socks, toys, and personal-care items to ship to the Philippines. Operation Care was a labor of love that enabled me to walk passionately in God's purpose for my life. The outreach ministry cared for countless homeless individuals in Dallas, and now it would reach into the country of my birth.

Operation Care gave me strength of purpose—it emotionally and spiritually supported me. I finished my work in the warehouse that day with barely enough time to rush home, shower and leave for my other full-time job, the one that financially supported me. Unfortunately, the drive to work allowed me to once again think about the disappointment I felt from my friend's inability to help at the warehouse. The sadness in my spirit returned. I was already tired and my evening shift had yet to begin as I pulled into our underground parking lot at the Collins Building. I prayed aloud as I parked my car.

"God, please encourage my heart. Give me supernatural strength this evening to take care of the people inside. And help me take care of the people outside as well. The people without shelter, clothing, or food—the people you have called me, and Operation Care to help. Lord, I need to know I'm doing what you want me to do."

How like God to answer a heartfelt prayer in a miraculous way.

It took three seconds (count with me, one, two, three …) and then my cell phone rang. This was very strange. I was in an underground parking structure, a place where cell phone service was typically nonexistent. When I answered, the voice on the other end of the line was crystal-clear.

"Hi Susie, this is Dianne. I know you're probably at the hospital, so I won't keep you, but I had to let you know that the donation we were praying for will be mailed today!"

I'm sure my voice could be heard throughout the parking structure, as I joyfully shouted.

"Yippee! Thank you, Lord! Thank you, thank you, thank you! You are awesome!"

We didn't know the amount of the donation from our beloved couple, only that it was "significant."

My shift that evening flew by, as did the weeks leading up to our trip to the Philippines.

Operation Care Philippines was a resounding success. We introduced the AWANA program to seven churches, and now hundreds of precious kids are in the loving care of these churches where they grow and learn about God and His Word. The kids are being trained to memorize Scripture and to love God with all their hearts. Our prayer is to equip these kids to become future leaders in the Philippines. On that trip, we reached over 2,000 young people between the ages of six and fourteen, and 1,704 Filipino slum kids accepted Jesus on that outreach. We even sent two children with cleft palate deformity to surgery! One of them is now in college, living a healthy life and serving the Lord through their church. Our theme that year was *Changing Lives, Changing the World.* There isn't a doubt in my mind that we did just that—and God made it possible!

Oh, and just in case you are wondering about the donation our faithful couple felt called to make—it was $25,000. Exactly what we needed when we needed it the most. And, as long as God continues to direct our path, provide bountiful blessings, and perform His outrageous miracles, we will continue in our efforts to be faithful servants and praise His Holy Name.

Mastering a Miracle Mindset

1. One measure of our likeness to Christ is our sensitivity to the suffering of others. Have you done anything lately to help "the least of these?"
2. God fulfills everything you need in accordance to His will. How have you known God is using you when things happen the right away?
3. Have you done something that took a lot of faith to do?

What is your miracle mindset for today?

_____

_____

_____

A beautiful decoration at the
Dallas Convention Center.

DAY 9

A Decorator Is Delivered

And whatever we ask we receive from Him,
because we keep His commandments and
do the things that are pleasing in His sight.
1 John 3:22 (NASB)

One month before our inaugural Christmas party for the homeless, the chairperson of our Decoration Committee resigned due to health issues and her doctor's recommendation. This was a serious problem because she wasn't just the chairperson, she was also the only person on the committee. We were planning the city's largest Christmas party at the Dallas Convention Center. We weren't talking about arranging color coordinated linens and table centerpieces—this was about decorating 100,000 square feet for a Christmas celebration for 10,000 people.

"Lord, you've got to handle this." I said earnestly. "*Please send us another decorator!*"

I had faith that God would give us another person. So I prayed and left it at the foot of the cross. Prayer and faith, they go hand in hand. You cannot have one without the other.

Exactly two weeks before the event I got a call from a lady named Donna Winborn who wanted to volunteer in the children's section. We had more than enough volunteers for that area, but I never want to turn down an offer to help. Suddenly, the Lord reminded me of the Decoration Committee, or rather the lack of a Decoration Committee. We still needed someone to be in charge of that area and coordinate the volunteers. I had spent several minutes talking to this gracious lady, and I was thinking that perhaps she could be an answer to prayer.

"We have a lot of volunteers signed up for the children's outreach, but if that's where you feel the Lord is calling you to help I'm sure we can find something." I said. "However, what we really need is someone to help with decorations. I'm afraid we lost the chairman of our Decoration Committee to a sudden illness, and this has left us with a tremendous void. But I'll be honest with you, we don't just need someone to help, we need someone to be in charge of this." I held my breath and prayed that she would be receptive to the invitation.

I could hear laughter on the other end of the phone and the Holy Spirit prodded me to ask a question.

"Donna, what do you do for a living?"

"I own a flower, plant, and tree company called L'amour Lesfleur. In fact, I decorate my own church and also another mega church in the area every Christmas season. I didn't ask if you needed help with decorations because I figured you probably had that under control already."

"Well, we didn't—but we do now, if you'll be our chairperson!" I joyfully exclaimed.

"It would be an honor," she said.

How like God to go above and beyond! He didn't just send us someone to decorate, He sent the owner of a professional decoration company. Donna and her team decked the "hall" for our first Operation Care Christmas Gift 2004, and it was spectacular! Her Christmas wonderland set the stage for an annual event that is now billed as the Nation's Largest Christmas Party—an event birthed in prayer and blessed with countless miracle memories. God will help us accomplish all that He asks us to do, and then some!

MASTERING A MIRACLE MINDSET

1. Have you ever faced a need so huge that only a miracle could provide the answer?
2. Do you pray about every situation believing that God will make a way?
3. Are you praying today, in faith, that God will help you accomplish something that He has clearly asked you to do?

PS: Hey, can I let you in on a secret? God has given us another vision to expand our annual event into a nation-wide outreach. Operation Care International is taking its program model for broad-based community evangelism, prayer, and foot washing, into every state in the country! Our goal is to initiate the World's Largest Christmas Party on December 19, 2020 where events just like ours held at the Dallas Convention Center will be held simultaneously in fifty states and other countries. Contact Operation Care International for more information on how your city can participate in **World Celebrates Jesus 2020.**

opcare.org

Barbers busy serving at the Haircut Station.

DAY 10

WANTED—TWENTY-FIVE BARBERS!

And whatever you ask in My name, that I will do,
that the Father may be glorified in the Son.
JOHN 14:13 (NKJV)

It was one week before the Nation's Largest Christmas Party for the Homeless at the Dallas Convention Center, and we still needed barbers. Our goal was to have twenty-five stations where professional barbers and hairdressers would cut the hair of hundreds of our guests. We were praying earnestly for this need, knowing that God would answer this prayer in a miraculous way. I honestly wasn't worried about it at all. I left it in God's hands, and I knew He would do what needed to be done in His time and in His way. After all, He had already coordinated so much, and everything was coming together!

The party would provide thousands of homeless people with food, clothing, personal-care items, sleeping bags, and blankets. There would be free medical, dental, and vision assessments. In addition to the haircuts, facials, and makeovers, a major aspect of this outreach was foot washing and the provision of new socks and shoes. We were also offering free phone calls, so our guests could contact family members, and if needed, we would even take them to the bus station and send them home to be reunited with their families.

The personal-care stations were important in lifting the morale of the homeless. We called places that we thought could help us like salons, barbershops, even hairdressing schools, but we didn't have any response. Exactly two days before the event we got a call from a gentleman.

"I've got several students who would like to volunteer to cut hair," he said.

"That is wonderful!" One of our volunteer coordinators asked, "How many students will be coming?"

"Twenty-five," he replied.

God is pleased to provide—especially when we approach Him with unwavering faith.

The hair grooming section was bursting with activity on that day. Although many men and women were transformed outwardly, it was the inward change that filled the room with the Spirit of God's love. There is a greeting card saying that attests, "Life is not measured by the number of breaths you take but by the moments that take your breath away." Seeing the countless transformations that day was one of those moments. For many of our special guests, their haircut was the outward manifestation of a profound inward transformation, as hearts and souls were meeting Jesus in a very real and very personal way.

MASTERING A MIRACLE MINDSET
1. Do you believe that God is never, ever late?
2. Is anything too big, or too little, to merit God's attention?
3. When was the last time God did something that took your breath away?

Adelfa Lorilla and Susie Jennings praising God together.

DAY 11

OUT OF BROKENNESS THE VISION APPEARED

Your sons and daughters will prophesy, your young men will see visions, your old men will dream dreams.
ACTS 2:17 (NIV)

Being in any type of outreach ministry is hard work. I was really getting discouraged and frustrated. The enemy kept telling me that Operation Care Dallas, a homeless ministry I founded, did not really make a difference in anyone's life. Yes, we saw thousands of people make professions of faith in Jesus Christ since the birth of the ministry in 1993. And, yes, that number had increased dramatically since Operation Care Christmas Gift 2004, our inaugural holiday event for the homeless that had grown into the Nation's Largest Christmas Party.

However, at that moment I couldn't think of a single person whose life was definitely changed because of the ministry of Operation Care. I knew within my heart that I was called to help the homeless, but that day all I felt called to do was quit. When Adelfa Lorilla, my office manager and assistant came to work at 9:00 that morning, I shared my discouragement and frustration with her. Adelfa is also a good friend who is like a sister to me. We both knelt down and started to pray together as we normally did every morning. However, it wasn't normal that I was feeling so depressed, that my heart was so sad. I cried out to the Lord to let me know if we were really making a difference and to encourage my heart about the effectiveness of the ministry. I told the Lord how sorry I was that we had not really contributed to anyone's life truly being changed for God's Kingdom—and I asked Him to forgive me. I wept and so did Adelfa.

Upon finishing our prayers, I stood up, raised my hands above my head with a worshipful attitude, and with my eyes still closed, I praised God for the peace He gave me. He lifted my burdens and took my sadness away. It was during this time of worship that I had a vision. I saw a beautiful spacious palace shining brightly with a large wide-open outer patio. There was a staircase on the patio, and I saw hundreds of men and women at the foot of the steps facing each other, standing shoulder to shoulder. They were all wearing white. A lady was walking in the middle of the crowd. She looked like royalty. She was wearing a white satin long-sleeved flowing gown with piping on the sleeves. As she walked, I got a glimpse of her face, and I recognized that it was me! This vision made me cry. Suddenly, the Spirit of the Lord spoke to my heart.

Susie, these are the people who have been saved because of Operation Care's ministry.

And then I felt a miraculous peace—a marked lightness in my spirit. When at last I could speak, I immediately told Adelfa what I saw.

"I saw almost the same vision!" Adelfa exclaimed. "People were lined up in the street facing each other, but instead of just walking through the crowd, you were shaking their hands!"

For a few moments, it was hard for either of us to speak.

We were overwhelmed with emotion and the realization of the answered prayer miracle we had just experienced together. Our shared vision was the confirmation I needed and an immense encouragement to my heart.

After that day, I did not doubt what God was doing in the life of Operation Care. He was making a difference, one life at a time, and thousands of people would be changed on earth and for eternity. We may never see all the fruit of our labor on earth—but we can rest assured that God knows. I don't need accolades here on earth; I just want to get to Heaven and hear God say, "Well done, my good and faithful servant."

"Well done, good and faithful servant! You have been faithful with a few things; I will put you in charge of many things. Come and share your master's happiness!"
(MATT. 25:21 NIV)

MASTERING A MIRACLE MINDSET

1. Have you ever let failure or disappointment cause you to doubt your call to serve God?
2. What do you think is the purpose of brokenness in a person's life?
3. How do you develop the sensitivity to really hear God's voice?

WHAT IS YOUR MIRACLE MINDSET FOR TODAY?

_____

_____

_____

My dear friend, Beth Lira.

DAY 12

Diagnosis: Stage 4 Cancer!

And the prayer of faith will save the sick,
and the Lord will raise him up.
James 5:14 (NKJV)

Let me tell you about my friend Beth. She was a very private person. But she was also very kind, generous, thoughtful, sensitive to the needs of others, and had shown so much love towards my elderly mom. Beth Lira was my classmate in college for three years while we were in nursing school at the Central Philippine University in the Philippines. She worked in California as a nurse while I worked in Dallas, Texas. I saw her during our class reunion in Chicago in 1990 and in California in the following year.

Every December we have a big Christmas Party for the homeless in Dallas. We usually serve about 10,000 homeless and impoverished families by providing for their physical and spiritual needs. It's a big event with an equally big budget. In December of 2005, I vividly remember when I received a thick brown envelope from Beth. To my amazement, it was filled with at least thirty checks all from different people in amounts ranging from ten to twenty dollars each. I was so touched that I cried. What an incredible gesture of love and compassion for the poor and the homeless. And oh how much it meant to me! I didn't wait for my tears to dry and immediately called to thank her.

"Beth, this is amazing! It has brought me so much encouragement. Thank you!" I said.

"I am working at two different hospitals now," she said, "and I did what you did when you started your ministry I asked my co-workers for donations to help Operation Care Dallas."

That was the beginning of Beth's yearly Christmas gift. Every December an envelope of checks would arrive from California. I was happy to hear her voice when she called one Saturday night to talk, until the tone of the conversation shifted.

"Susie, I was just diagnosed with Stage 4 ovarian cancer. I need your help."

She learned of her cancer the previous Wednesday and had been so sick ever since that she could not eat or even lie flat on her back because of excruciating abdominal pain.

"I called because of the note you sent to me about your total abdominal hysterectomy in 2004. After seeing my doctor, I was doing some research and your one-page letter fell out."

When I had several endometriomas removed and experienced a completely painless post-operative recovery from surgery, I wrote to her about the miracle—knowing that as a fellow nurse she would appreciate how rare—and miraculous it was.

"Susie, I'm scheduled to have surgery this Wednesday," she said quietly.

My heart went out to Beth. I felt so much love and compassion for this precious sister in Christ. We talked about Jesus and heaven and eternity. I didn't talk to her about death, but I was so happy to know that Beth was saved and had accepted Jesus into her heart—that if anything did happen in surgery and that she would be with our Lord and Savior and that I would see her again one day.

"Let me pray for your complete healing!" I said, and proceeded to cry out to God with all my heart. I was so heart-broken because I cared deeply for Beth. I also knew that she was not the type who could easily ask for help. I asked God to take away her pain and sustain her. After we hung up, I continued to pray for Beth. I felt in my spirit that God was going to heal her.

"God, I know you specialize in miracles—please bring us a miracle and heal Beth!" I prayed.

The next day she called again.

"It was amazing, Susie." She said. "After your prayer last night, I was able to drink tea for the first time in days and I could lay flat on my back!"

"Praise Jesus!" I said. "I just know God is going to heal you! Please, can I pray for you every night until your surgery?"

She was very grateful and accepted my offer without hesitation. So every night Beth and I would pray together. She would wait for my phone call after my evening shift at the hospital. I prayed with expectation for God to do a miracle in Beth's life so she could testify to her friends and family as to the miraculous power of prayer.

Thankfully, she was able to do just that, because God did answer our prayer! Her surgery went very well and we prayed her through it. God healed Beth for a long season and gave her another three years. In her last days, she was so in love with Jesus that she was passionate in sharing

Him with the world. She was planting the seeds of faith by sharing Jesus with virtually everyone she met. Beth was such an inspiration! I believe that was the reason God answered our prayers for healing so that others could hear and know Christ.

My sweet friend Beth left a legacy of love and faith when she left this earthly realm. But the sadness I felt was brief as I rest in the comfort of knowing we will be together for eternity when I join her in heaven one day.

Mastering a Miracle Mindset

If you have experienced being with a person you love when he or she received bad news you know it can be hard to know what to say. How can God use us to be a miracle in the lives of those we care about who are going through tough times?

What is your miracle mindset for today?

_____

_____

_____

Part Three

MIRACLES OF GOD'S PERFECT TIMING

Lots of happy children in India.

DAY 13

The Birth of Operation Care India 2009

*Whatever you do, do your work heartily, as for the Lord
rather than for men, knowing that from the Lord you
will receive the reward of the inheritance.
It is the Lord Christ whom you serve.*
Colossians 3:23-24 (NASB)

It was a Sunday evening, and I was speaking at a church in Mesquite, Texas, giving my testimony. After the service, someone introduced me to Mike Relton, a man from India, who it turned out was also a member of my own church.

"Please, you must meet my wife; she needs to hear your testimony."

"I would love to meet her," I looked around but didn't see a woman nearby, "please bring her over."

"She is not here, but our house is just five minutes away; would you accept my invitation to come over now?"

Although I'm an outgoing person and always ready to talk about Jesus and what He has done in my life and in the development of Operation Care, I'm not in the habit of following strangers to their home. I was ready to decline as gracefully as possible when I began to feel a very strong prompting from the Holy Spirit and the next thing I knew I was in my car following him home to meet his wife.

She didn't appear surprised to see that her husband had

invited a guest home from church. He introduced us and quickly walked out of the room.

"I will be right back," he said.

"I know you!" Grace Relton said as she shook my hand and asked me to sit down. "I have seen you in church. Now I know why I cleaned my house today! I never clean on Sunday, but when I came home from church God spoke in my heart to clean it. He knew I was going to have a visitor."

When he returned, Mike was holding some loose photos and a book. He sat down next to me.

"I have something to show you. These are all pictures from India." He showed me many photos of children and pointed to one where a large group of children were sitting in the front row of a church raising their hands.

"These children accepted Jesus as their savior during the time of invitation."

"Are you a minister?" I asked.

"My husband is an evangelist for the Lord," his wife said.

Mike shuffled through the stack of photos and handed one to me.

"Is that you?" I exclaimed as I stared at the mind-boggling scene.

"Yes." He said quietly. "That is me."

I could only shake my head in amazement.

It turns out Mike Relton was Dr. Mike Relton, a theologian and evangelist who God was using to reach literally tens of thousands of people in his native country. The photo showed him preaching in front of thousands of people that stretched as far as you could see—like sand on a seashore. As I looked at the photo and then at Mike and his sweet wife, the Holy Spirit spoke to me in a very loud and clear fashion.

You are going to India to help the poor and needy kids.

It didn't appear as though Mike or his wife had heard the same prompting, and I was debating whether to share my revelation with them when Mike showed me the book in his hands.

"I would like to give you a copy of my book. It is about prayer."

I took the book and opened it randomly. The title of the prayer on the page I opened to took my breath away, it was called: *A Prayer for the Homeless*. I am seldom speechless, but the number of confirmations the Lord was providing made me quite emotional.

"I knew God had something special planned tonight," Mike said. "I didn't know what it was until I heard you speak. Then I knew. This is a divine appointment," he declared.

He proceeded to tell me that the day before he and his wife took the wrong exit off the highway. While turning around, they saw an unfamiliar church they didn't even know was there. That evening, Mike was driving to another church when he heard the Holy Spirit tell him to go to the church they discovered when they had made the wrong turn. As a strong spirit-filled believer, Mike made it a point to listen and obey God's prompting and so he drove to that church instead—where I was speaking.

"When I heard you speak tonight about your story and your ministry and God's amazing faithfulness in your life and the miracles He has provided, I knew that He wanted us to meet—to talk—about my country—about India."

And so it goes … another miracle in a growing orchard of miracles that is bearing the wholesome fruit of salvation. Mike's unconditional obedience led to the birth of Operation Care India, where in July of 2009 we ministered to over 2,000 mostly Hindu homeless and slum children. When we shared the gospel message with these precious souls hungry for God's love, 1,997 children accepted Jesus as their Lord and Savior! And just think . . . this miracle all began with a wrong turn.

MASTERING A MIRACLE MINDSET

1. Do you believe that, with God, there are no accidents?
2. Have you ever found yourself feeling lost, only to realize that God was actually redirecting your path? His ways are not our ways, and often the best way to experience a miracle moment is to trust God's plan.

WHAT IS YOUR MIRACLE MINDSET FOR TODAY?

_____

_____

_____

Chaplain Nate Wilson, Dr. Satish Rao and Peter Friedlander.

DAY 14

The Doctor Sent by God

*The LORD sustains them on their sickbed and restores
them from their bed of illness.*
Psalm 41:3 (NIV)

Anyone who has traveled internationally knows how challenging it can sometimes be to acclimate to changes in time, weather, elevation, language, and culture—just to name a few. However, one of the greatest challenges in visiting a new country is often those associated with dietary changes. A difference in food types, preparation, and particularly in water can often cause uncomfortable digestive distress. Such was the case during our Operation Care trip to India in July 2009, when most of our team became ill shortly after our arrival. Whether it was food-related or a "bug" we picked up on the long flight was unclear, but we had back-to-back events scheduled over the next few days beginning the first night we arrived, and we didn't have the luxury of taking it easy until we felt better. We prayed for healing and did everything pro-active we could think of.

When it was time to head out for our first event that evening, most of us felt better, or at least stronger except for Nate Wilson, our beloved chaplain, who was so ill he had to stay behind in our hotel. He had some abdominal discomfort, vomiting and severe diarrhea.

"There's no way I can make it," he said. "But I'll be praying for you, and I'm hoping I will feel better soon."

We hated to leave him, but he reminded us of our mission and of the thousands of people who would be introduced to the hope and healing of our Lord Jesus.

That evening when we returned from our event, the owner of the hotel was waiting anxiously for us in the entrance.

"Your chaplain is very ill," she said.

"Have you called a doctor?" I asked.

"No, there is no one to call. You must take him to the hospital now."

A few of us rushed to Nate's room, and indeed he wasn't doing very well. He wasn't on death's doorstep, but he clearly felt miserable. He couldn't keep anything in his stomach and as a nurse I could see he was dangerously dehydrated.

"We need to pray now," I said to the team members in the room.

"Lord, we need a miracle right now! Please heal Nate so he does not have to be hospitalized. You know that our biggest event is tomorrow and we need our chaplain! Lord, You did not bring him this far to leave him here." I asked—begged—for God's help.

I was on my way downstairs to see what I could find for Nate to drink when the Holy Spirit reminded me of the tea I brought with me from Dallas. I don't even drink tea regularly, but while I was packing, something prompted me to toss the teabags into my suitcase. I took him a cup and he was able to drink it without vomiting. This was a good sign. I was heading back to my room to get more tea bags for him to drink later when I heard the owner's son calling my name as he was climbing the stairs. Our rooms were on the second and third floors.

"Susie, there is a doctor on the phone for you!"

When I got to the phone, it turned out this had nothing whatsoever to do with Nate—at least not at first. This doctor was the friend of Dr. Janet Merrill, one of our missionaries in Dallas. I recall Janet telling me that she would contact a friend of hers who lived in India to let him know we would be in his city so that we would have a "local" nearby who could perhaps lend a hand if needed. When he introduced himself as Dr. Satish Rao, I assumed because of the connection with Janet that he was most likely a doctor of theology.

"Mrs. Jennings, I am sorry it has taken me so long to contact you. Our mutual friend in your country, Dr. Janet, sent me this email ten days ago, but I only just opened it tonight. I called you as soon as I read the message. I wanted to let you know that I live nearby in New Delhi and to give you my phone number in case there is something I can help with while you and your team are here."

I looked at the clock, it was 9:30 PM. I suddenly felt prompted to ask a question.

"What kind of a doctor are you?" I asked.

"A medical doctor; I have a practice here in New Delhi."

"Thank you, Jesus!" I shouted into the air and quickly proceeded to tell him of our medical emergency and what a miracle it was that he called.

Our doctor from heaven arrived less than one hour later. He examined our sick teammate as we waited and prayed. He looked hopeful when he was finished with the exam, but wasted no time as he headed quickly down the stairs.

"I am going out to get the medicine he needs. I will return immediately. Your friend will be fine. The tea is good; see if he can drink more."

It was shortly after midnight when Dr. Rao—our doctor sent by God—returned and administered the medicine Chaplain Nate desperately needed. We all had a very long day in front of us, and we retired to our rooms to pray and try to get some sleep. It should have come as no surprise that Chaplain Nate was the first one to arrive for our devotional time at 5:30 that morning.

"I feel like a new person!" he declared.

That day, Chaplain Nate joined us as an integral part of the Operation Care India team for the big event where over a thousand children responded to the gospel presentation. It had been a harrowing twenty-four hours, but God in His infinite wisdom had everything under control and timed perfectly. After all, He is the miracle healer.

MASTERING A MIRACLE MINDSET

Think back to a time when God answered a specific prayer very quickly. Did you see that as a miracle moment? If not, do you think you may in the future?

WHAT IS YOUR MIRACLE MINDSET FOR TODAY?

_____

_____

_____

All smiles with no pain!
With my gynecologist, Dr. James Norwood.

DAY 15

A Surgery, Painless Postoperatively

If you worship me, the LORD your God, I will bless you with food and water and take away all your sicknesses.
Exodus 23:25 (GNT)

As a full-time recovery room nurse supervisor at one of the busiest surgical centers in Dallas, I saw doctors all the time. However, I always put off actually "seeing" a doctor for my own health concerns until it was absolutely necessary. By mid-January of 2004, that time came.

In retrospect, that I had managed to make it through the busy Christmas season was nothing short of a miracle. Yes, I had pain off and on, but I was extremely busy working full-time and also planning two Operation Care Christmas events. I didn't have time to be sick.

The Birthday Bash for Jesus on December 13 was a great success, and we shared the gospel and delivered 1,000 blankets to the homeless on the streets of Dallas. Twenty-two homeless men and women accepted Jesus as Savior. The following week on December 20, we were also able to provide approximately 10,000 toys and books to the poorest kids in Dallas at the annual Edie Clark Christmas Party, an event we agreed to organize at the last minute at the request of my church. From that outreach, 153 accepted Jesus as Lord. All told, this was one of my best Christmases ever—in spite of the nagging pain! I'm sure God had everything to do with my ability to see both of those events to fruition before I could no longer ignore the increasing pain in my abdomen, hip, and groin.

I was diagnosed with severe Ovarian Endometriomas on January 27, 2004, on what would have been my late husband's fifty-second birthday. By then, he had been gone for eleven years, but the "coincidence" of the date wasn't lost on me. What I had was a sub-type of endometriosis characterized by painful cysts, I actually had five endometriomas, and one was about 9 cm—roughly the size of a small cantaloupe. They scheduled my surgery for early February.

The day of my surgery, I held the hands of my surgeon and anesthesiologist and prayed with them before the attendant wheeled me into the operating room on a stretcher. I praised God's Holy Name up until I faded into drug-induced oblivion after my anesthesiologist asked me to count backwards from ten to one. My "exploratory" surgery ended up being very extensive and included a total abdominal hysterectomy.

"I'll be honest with you, Susie," my surgeon said when he talked to me, "this was one of the worst cases I've seen. The tumors were embedded in your internal organs like super glue."

"Well, you know me, Doctor," I mumbled through post-anesthesia grogginess, "I may be small, but I have to do things in a big way."

They usually give a grade level to the severity of a case from 0—4, and my case was a 4+.

I did not ask God why I had the tumors or such a severe case, but I did ask Him how I could use this situation to glorify His name. The answer was my miraculous recovery. Four hours after surgery, I was sitting up in a chair, and twenty hours later, I took a shower with no assistance and walked four times in one day. I had a co-worker, a nurse, who wrote in my guestbook. "Susie, you are a true follower of your God. It is showing in your amazing recovery."

The best part was that I did not experience pain after surgery. I was in the hospital for three days with no need for pain medication and was pain-free in my recovery at home. And thankfully, all of the tumors were benign. No tumor is too big that God cannot heal. No problem is too large that God cannot solve. No pain is too severe that God cannot ease.

Has God called you to do something that you thought was impossible? It's so exciting to see what God has in store for us if we listen for His voice and exercise unconditional obedience when we hear Him. Nothing is too big for the Lord if you give it to Him. Honor God and He will honor you!

MASTERING A MIRACLE MINDSET

If you have ever been diagnosed with a serious illness, did it make you feel closer to God or further away from God? What possible miracle moments can come from pain and suffering?

WHAT IS YOUR MIRACLE MINDSET FOR TODAY?

_____

_____

_____

A life changing experience for the children.

DAY 16

A Colorful Lesson of Conviction

I have blotted out, like a thick cloud, your
transgressions, and like a cloud, your sins.
Return to Me, for I have redeemed you.
Isaiah 44:22 (NKJV)

We were in India, and I was about to speak through an interpreter to 500 Hindu and Muslim children. I looked out at a sea of young impressionable children who were waiting with great anticipation to hear what this stranger from another country was going to say. Most of them lived nearby in the slums, close to the trash dumping areas.

"Let me tell you what the colors mean on the bracelets we just handed out. Is everyone wearing their bracelet?" I held my hand in the air to display my own bracelet and smiled as many of the children waved their hands in the air to show me theirs. But something puzzled me.

We had 500 children; we brought 600 bracelets, and I could see the box was empty, but I noticed that some kids didn't have one. After years as a supervising nurse in the recovery room of a major medical center, I was accustomed to sizing up emergencies and thinking fast. It didn't take long to assess what was going on as I noticed some kids poking others with their elbows, others reaching slyly into their pockets, and some looking away in guilt and shame. I asked the Lord for guidance, and His response was immediate.

Use the balloons for an illustration.

There were colorful balloons with ribbon tails all around the room that replicated the five colors in our salvation bracelets.

I asked some team members to each grab a different color balloon and join me up front. As they did that, I addressed the children.

"I can see that some of you don't have bracelets, but I think we can fix that! Does everyone want to help me do that?" I clapped my hands and nodded with excitement as the children joyfully followed suit.

"Okay! Let's get started!" I waved my hand to show the beaded bracelet around my own wrist.

"This is called a salvation bracelet, because each color has a special meaning to illustrate a part of the Gospel of Jesus." As I explained each color, I pointed to the team member holding the balloon in the same color.

"Let's start with black. Black represents sin. Sin is when you do something wrong, like tell a lie, disobey your parents, quarrel with others, or if you take something that is not yours, that is sin. Being unkind is sin."

I pointed at the red balloon. "Red stands for the blood of Jesus. We need the blood of Jesus to wash away sins because Jesus gave His life for our sin." I explained this in a little more detail as I walked toward the team member holding the white balloon.

"White represents what happens to our heart when Jesus washes away our sins! It becomes like new! It is clean!"

"Green is about growing up God's way. We all want to do that, right?" The children shouted yes and cheered.

"And yellow . . . yellow is the promise of Heaven where

there are streets of gold! If we have accepted Jesus Christ as Lord and Savior, we have the promise of a home in Heaven."

I walked to the person holding the black balloon and took it from them. I looked at the balloon with disgust and held it as far away from me as I could. I lowered my voice and spoke more seriously.

"Sin is a very bad thing. It keeps us separated from all the wonderful colors of God's love!" I pointed at all of the colorful balloons. "Sometimes we don't realize what we have done is sin, but then we feel something inside of our heart that tells us we did something wrong, and that is called "conviction." For example, if you took an extra bracelet, that is sin. It does not belong to you, and it is unkind to the children who did not get one. That is the color black! You need to return it, and say 'No!' to sin!" I released the black balloon. "Jesus will wash your sins and will make your heart clean and white as snow so you can grow the right way and one day walk on streets of gold in Heaven! Does anyone feel conviction in their heart?"

As soon as I said those words, many children raised their hands and started returning the missing bracelets. They could not get the extra bracelets they had taken out of their pockets fast enough. It was such a joy to see the Holy Spirit convicting the precious hearts of these kids.

Soon, every child in the room had a bracelet.

"When you wear your bracelet you can remember what all of the colors represent." I said. "And somebody might even ask you about it and then you will be able to share the love of Jesus Christ with someone else! Isn't that exciting?" Their energy and enthusiasm was contagious as they shouted for joy and clapped.

"If you want to accept Jesus in your heart as your Lord

and Savior, please stand up!" My heart was full of emotion as I invited them into the family of God. Every child in the room stood up.

"All you have to do is repeat after me . . . " I spoke the words as the interpreter translated them after me.

It was a sight to behold as the children stood up and their beautiful voices merged to say the sinner's prayer in unison. It was a spectacular occurrence to see those children bowing their heads and praying to the One True God!

I knew many of the children had taken more bracelets than they should have, and I could have admonished them for their wrongdoing and forced or shamed them into admission. But to what end would that have served? True conviction needs to start inside our heart when we know we have done wrong and truly desire to change—not because someone tells us we have done wrong and forces us to change. I thank God Almighty that on that day He gave me a colorful lesson of conviction that helped me show these precious children the love of Christ. Once again, God's perfect timing was—perfect! I would like to think the miracle of addressing a wrong action in the right way made the miracle of salvation all the sweeter.

Mastering a Miracle Mindset

1. What is your natural reaction when someone does something wrong? Do you get angry? Confront them? Tell someone else? Or turn the other way and ignore it?

2. How can you be a miracle in the life of someone who has sinned?

3. What positive action can you take that might help a sinner feel the inner conviction to repent and make right the wrong?

What is your miracle mindset for today?

_____

_____

_____

My friends after their release from customs detention.

DAY 17

Give Us One More Hour!

*Could you men not keep watch with
me for one hour? He asked Peter.*
Luke 22:40

Our team of twelve for Operation Care Holy Land 2014 arrived at the airport in Tel Aviv Ben-Gurion, Israel at 11:45 PM on July 4, 2014. It was Independence Day in the United States, and after being cooped up in planes and airport terminals far longer than originally anticipated, we were celebrating freedom as well, as we disembarked from the final flight of our journey.

We were all excited about the twenty events planned for the next ten days in Israel and Jordan. We praised God that He brought us here safely to help countless children in Jerusalem, Nazareth, Netanya, and Bethlehem, as well as thousands of Syrian refugee children in Jordan.

However, it had been a very long day, and we were exhausted. We started in Dallas very early that morning and changed planes in New York. We were taxiing down the runway in New York, headed for Moscow, when bad weather hit, and we were delayed for three hours on the tarmac before our departure. Then, we had a five-hour layover in Moscow before boarding another plane to this, our final destination: Tel Aviv. We were going through customs when one of our team members, Safeeya, was ushered into another room for questioning. We were aware this might happen because she was born in Kuwait. Fortunately, Safeeya's husband, David, was permitted to stay with her.

"Don't worry," I said, as they were separated from our group, "we will get our luggage and wait for both of you."

This little glitch would not dampen our spirits. We didn't know how long it would take for Safeeya to clear customs and join us with David, but we were a team and unanimously voted to wait. While getting our luggage, I saw our tour guide from Plano arrive on another flight. Rani Espanioly was supposed to arrive ahead of us but he, too, got delayed, which I believe was God's plan.

"Safeeya is being detained," I told him, "and we are still waiting on the rest of our luggage to come down."

Rani had led many trips to the Holy Land and was an experienced tour guide. He quickly took charge and helped our team retrieve our luggage from the carousel. Unfortunately, all of our luggage didn't arrive. Brian and Julie were missing four bags, as were David and Safeeya. Brenda and I were each missing one bag. All told, ten pieces of luggage were missing—and still in Moscow we soon learned.

"You're going to have to fill out some paperwork," Rani said to me, "so how about if I take the rest of the team and their luggage out to the bus, okay? We could wait for you there."

Everyone agreed that was a good idea.

"You go with them, honey," Brian said to his wife Julie. "I'll file the report for our bags and stay here with Susie to wait for Safeeya and David."

"We will wait for you outside," Julie said.

"Is your phone with you, Susie?" Rani asked me.

"Yes, but it needs to be charged."

"Give it to me, please," he said, and proceeded to plug a cord into a nearby outlet and recharge my phone.

Rani and the team went to the bus, and we filed the necessary reports to locate and retrieve our missing luggage. Brian and I prayed with great expectations that every piece of luggage would be delivered to our hotel in a timely manner. Then we waited inside the airport for David and Safeeya, while the team waited outside on the tour bus with Rani, the driver, and the owner of the tour company, Andre. Over two hours passed when my cell phone rang, and I was so thankful that Rani had thought to charge it for me.

"Has there been any news?" Rani asked. "Should I take the team to the hotel?"

"Give us one more hour," I said. "I feel in my spirit that David and Safeeya will be released any moment."

Brian and I prayed fervently that this would indeed be the case. The airport was almost empty as I walked through the concourse claiming God's power over the enemy. I stood in the middle of the airport near the entrance, raised my hands and prayed loud for the Lord to help us. I did not care whether someone saw me.

"Lord, please let them release Safeeya! Bring her and David back to our team, so we can do the work You have called us here to do!"

Less than ten minutes later, Rani called.

"Safeeya has been released from questioning!" he informed me. "They just called me. The officials are checking her passport now, and you should see her and David soon."

I looked at my watch, it was exactly one hour from my last conversation with Rani when Safeeya emerged with David. I jumped out of my seat so fast and hugged her and David.

"You waited for us!" Safeeya said gratefully.

"Of course we did!" Brian and I said in unison.

"The entire team is still here; let's go join them on the bus!" I joyfully shouted.

"Thank you," David said, obviously relieved that his wife had been cleared, and they could breathe more freely. We would come to learn it was a very frightening experience. There was so much excitement on that lone tour bus in the empty parking lot in the wee hours of the morning as hugs, laughter, and loud praises to God filled the night air with joy.

"Thank you all so much for waiting for us" David and Safeeya were overwhelmed with emotion at this gesture of love.

"It was a united decision," everyone chimed. "And Cecille led us in a prayer meeting," Julie said. Cecille was one of our wonderful Operation Care board members.

"Thank you, Jesus!" I shouted to the heavens. "Thank you for this amazing team who is prayerful and united."

It was now a few hours before sunrise, and the weight of exhaustion was heavy on all of us, but the love that was present on that bus was light and refreshing, and we could feel the spirit and presence of God in a powerful way.

"Thank you, God," I said as I lifted my hands in praise, "for individually picking everyone on this team in order to work together and accomplish the mission you have given to us. We do it all for Your glory, God!" A hearty chorus of "Amens" accompanied the sound of the bus engine as the driver turned the key and we practically collapsed into our seats. It was almost 5:00 AM by the time we got to our hotel in Jerusalem and agreed to sleep for a few hours and meet in the lobby at 10:00 AM.

When our team united once again, the energy of anticipation was palpable as we agreed to be on the lookout for more miracles and answered prayers from God. We all felt certain that God was going to bless Operation Care Holy Land 2014 in a mighty way. This was only the beginning. He didn't let us down. By noon that day, all ten pieces of our missing luggage arrived at our hotel. And the miracles continued…

MASTERING A MIRACLE MINDSET

1. Do you really believe that God is able to "work together for good" all things for those who love Him?
2. What difficulties do you face today? What stands in the way of the success of your "mission?"
3. Can you trust God to work it out in a way that is good, even miraculous?

WHAT IS YOUR MIRACLE MINDSET FOR TODAY?

_____

_____

_____

Dr. W. A. Criswell and Susie.

DAY 18

Dr. W.A. Criswell and Me

Therefore, as we have opportunity,
let us do good to all people, especially to those
who belong to the family of believers.
Galatians 6:10 (NIV)

With over two decades in ministry, I've been blessed to have Christian leaders, scholars, and theologians pray for me and the vision God placed in my heart. However, Dr. W. A. Criswell was the first pastor I asked to bless Operation Care after we became an "official" nonprofit organization in 2001. We had been giving away blankets to the homeless in the Dallas Metroplex area since late 1993, but we were about to launch our first event as a formal nonprofit outreach. Our ambitious plan on the Saturday before Christmas was to give away 1,000 blankets at our first Birthday Bash for Jesus. A blessing from this well-respected man of God would mean so much to the ministry—and to me.

A world-renowned theologian and scholar, Dr. Criswell was an early pioneer of the modern mega church phenomenon. In 1944, he was called to replace George Washington Truett as the pastor of the First Baptist Church in Dallas. During his tenure, membership grew from 7,800 to 26,000, with weekly Sunday School attendance in excess of 5,000. The church expanded to multiple buildings covering five blocks in downtown Dallas, eventually becoming the largest Southern Baptist church in the world. Billy Graham joined the church in 1953, became a close friend of the Criswell family, and remained a member of the Dallas congregation for fifty-five years.

Dr. Criswell understood the need to integrate spirituality into daily life—not just on Sunday at church—and he introduced a number of innovations at First Baptist Dallas that became a model for growing churches all over the country. By the early 1950s, he had hired professionally-trained educational directors for each age group of the church, organized a sophisticated multilevel Sunday School program, added a full-time business manager to the staff, and broadened the church into a youth and family life center featuring a bowling alley, skating rink, and gymnasium with a track and basketball court. He greatly expanded the church's long-standing Silent Friends ministry, creating for the deaf their own Sunday School, Training Union, Vacation Bible School, and summer camp ministries.

His vigorous outreach efforts in the community included sponsoring thirty-seven inner-city missions, a crisis pregnancy center, the Good Shepherd and Dallas Life Foundation ministries for the homeless and disadvantaged, Spanish-language chapels, and extensive television and radio ministries. Church services were locally televised as early as January, 1951, and eventually were carried on stations nationwide.

This gifted man of God was awarded eight honorary doctorates in addition to his earned postgraduate degree. He published fifty-four books, founded both the First

Baptist Academy and both Criswell College with its radio station KCBI.

Pastor and author Rick Warren refers to Dr. Criswell as the "greatest American pastor of the twentieth century." I, however, call him *my* pastor, and it is the teaching, preaching, and inspiration of this legendary spiritual giant that God used to help me develop a listening heart of compassion. In many ways, God used Dr. W. A. Criswell to shape me into a messenger of God with a mission to serve Him. All told, Dr. Criswell preached more than four thousand sermons from the pulpit of First Baptist Dallas, many of which I personally experienced sitting in the pew as a member of his congregation. That is why a blessing from this well-respected man of God would mean so much to the ministry—and to me.

Welcome to America

I was working as a nurse in the Philippines in 1982 when Baylor University Medical Center recruited me and made it possible for me to come to the United States. I arrived in the country on Thursday, September 9, 1982. That Sunday I attended my first service at First Baptist Church in Dallas, and on Monday, September 13, I started my new job as a nurse at Baylor. I joined the church before the end of the year. In January of 1983, I met David Jennings, a long-time member of First Baptist (since the age of two), and in 1984 Dr. Criswell joyfully officiated at our marriage. Nine years later in 1993, he performed the funeral service when we buried my beloved David.

The Blessing

To be granted a private visit with Dr. Criswell in December, 2001, was a blessing itself, as he was in the last stages of cancer. It was only a matter of time before Jesus came to take him home. I arrived at my appointed time, grateful to have this rare opportunity. I was ushered to an area in the home that was converted into an efficient hospital room, where equipment, supplies, and medications were close by. The room was dark and quiet when I entered, and Dr. Criswell was lying on a recliner where he appeared comfortable. I sat next to him and reminded him who I was.

"It's Susie Jennings, pastor, the wife of David Jennings." He nodded with understanding.

"Since David died, I have been helping homeless people in our city," I said slowly. "God gave me a ministry called Operation Care, and we are going to have a Christmas party for Jesus and invite all of the homeless men, women and children in our community to attend."

His face lit up when he heard the word "Christmas."

"Dr. Criswell, we are going to give away 1,000 blankets and share the gospel with the homeless on the streets of Dallas." It appeared that he understood what I said, and seemed pleased with what he heard. I knelt down by the side of his chair and placed my hand on his.

"Pastor, I have come to ask if you would please bless me as I obey God's leading in my life to help the homeless. Our first event as an official nonprofit ministry is this Saturday, and I want to bless the name of the Lord with our Birthday Bash for Jesus. Please, would you pray for me and bless me?"

"Yes, of course," he said quietly and smiled.

I bowed my head as Dr. Criswell held my hand and started to pray. Even with my eyes closed I could suddenly *feel* an amazing light shining brightly around us. His words of praise and blessing were clear as they flowed from his lips, and I felt an immense peace engulf me. It was then I felt the presence of the Lord in that glorious room, and I looked up to see Dr. Criswell directing his prayer toward the foot of the recliner, as though Jesus was standing right there, and he was talking to Him like a trusted friend. He asked the Lord to bless me and our outreach to the homeless—to give me a double portion of His Spirit, love and favor. He prayed for a long time, and I was crying before he was done.

Never before or since have I felt the presence of the Almighty in such a profound way as I did that day when Dr. Criswell called upon the Lord and gave me and Operation Care his blessing. I walked from his room that day as if I was walking on air. To experience this mighty servant of God speak so boldly and yet so intimately to our Savior was extraordinary. It was also a confirmation that God had given me the mission, message, and passion to share His light and love through Operation Care—and that if I listen closely and obey unconditionally, everything He wants done will get done. To receive this blessing from my spiritual mentor and beloved pastor was more than a miracle; it was life changing.

A Beginning and an End

Our first Birthday Bash for Jesus was a phenomenal success. Operation Care had established itself as a "credible" nonprofit ministry, and God orchestrated countless miraculous moments in the lives of those we served. It was also clear that God had big plans for the lives of many of the volunteers and sponsors who felt called to join us on the servant journey. I knew from that point the outcome will never be in doubt. For it is written in Philippians 1:6, "being confident of this, that he who began a good work in you will carry it on to completion until the day of Christ Jesus" (NIV).

A few weeks later on January 10, 2002, Dr. Criswell passed quietly into the arms of His Lord and Savior. He was ninety-two years old. His death made national headlines, and as a farewell honor, the city of Dallas closed off the US 75, North Central Expressway, for the celebrated pastor's funeral procession. Although his earthly body is gone, the indelible imprint he left in the lives of countless generations will live forever. And I am one of those eternally grateful souls. Thank you, Dr. Criswell, for your wisdom and your blessing.

I believe another grateful soul is our current pastor and spiritual leader, Dr. Robert Jeffress, and he grew up under Pastor Criswell whom he cites as an influence on his own ministry. A truly anointed and gifted man of God, Dr. Robert Jeffress carries on the legacy of First Baptist Dallas with his courageous spirit, deep conviction, and inspiring passion in speaking the Word. He is a man who values Bible-centered preaching and teaching as the foundation for all that we do, and he guides our growing church family with wisdom and grace.

Just like Dr. Criswell, Dr. Jeffress also supports the Operation Care ministry, and he prays for me. When I ask him to pray before our annual Christmas event, His blessing is always very important. The entire staff and my church family at First Baptist Dallas are incredibly supportive, and I am forever grateful for their partnership. Together in our desire to share the Word of God and Jesus' love, we are all changing lives and changing the world, one life at a time.

Making a difference for eternity is our business!

I know Dr. Criswell is proud.

Mastering a Miracle Mindset

1. Think of someone who has influenced your life and stop to thank God for this person.
2. Look at the events in your life for times when something occurred that you cannot explain in words. Could this be a miracle from God?
3. What is going on in your life today that may seem out of place to you but could be God's perfect timing for the purpose He has for your life?

What is your miracle mindset for today?

_____

_____

_____

Part Four

MIRACLES OF OBEDIENCE

In flight - Best place to share Jesus.
They can't run or get off the plane.

DAY 19

One Said, No! The Other Said, Yes!

This is good and it pleases God our Savior, who wants everyone to be saved and to come to know the truth.
1 Timothy 2: 3-4 (GNT)

Every time I board a plane I ask God to seat me near someone with whom I can share the Lord. Planes are the best place to evangelize—you literally have a captive audience. The person you're talking to cannot jump from the plane or stay in the lavatory too long. I depend on God's Word to save souls, not on my own. Scripture says in Isaiah 55:11, "So is my word that goes out from my mouth: It will not return to me empty, but will accomplish what I desire and achieve the purpose for which I sent it."

On my flight that day, God sat me between two men. On my right was an elderly man and on my left was a teenager. I said hello to both and introduced myself. During take-off, I prayed silently and asked God who I should share Jesus with first, the man or the teenager. The impression I got was strong.

Begin with the man.

I established rapport with the elderly gentleman, and he told me he was a businessman. I engaged him in a conversation and upon discovering that he was not a believer,

I proceeded to share the gospel with him. As I neared the end of my message, I could sense our conversation had become increasingly one-sided. When I asked if he wanted to accept Jesus as his Savior and Lord, his answer was a very firm, "No." I was so disappointed that I did not want to share Jesus with the teenager. Besides, the young man's eyes were closed. So, I proceeded to talk to the Lord in my heart, as I often did.

Lord, I'm not going to share with the teenager. He's sleeping anyway, and we only have ten minutes before we land.

Just then, the teenager opened his eyes.

And I heard God's voice within my heart, "What will you say when you stand before Me on judgment day, and I ask you, 'Why did you not share Jesus with the teenager?'"

There's nothing quite like Holy Spirit conviction, and I immediately started a conversation with the young man. He wasn't interested in small talk.

"What do you do? Are you a preacher?" he asked.

"Oh gosh, no, I'm a nurse. And I do volunteer work for a homeless ministry, and I love to tell people about Jesus. He changed my life and gave me hope and happiness. I've seen Him change the lives of so many people—it's completely amazing."

"And He does that with, what did you call it . . . His gospel?"

The teenager I thought was sleeping had been listening to every word I shared with the hard-hearted man to my right. It turns out my message was for him all along. Before we landed, the sweet young man accepted Jesus as his Lord and Savior. What an opportunity I would have missed if I had not listened to the conviction of the Holy Spirit—another sky-high miracle.

Mastering a Miracle Mindset

1. How persistent are you in telling others about the good news of salvation in Christ? Remember, YOU could be the miracle in someone's life.

2. Do you realize that your duty as a believer is to simply share the Gospel and not to convert anyone? (That's the work of the Holy Spirit!)

3. What steps can you take to make you bolder and more prepared to share about Jesus?

What is your miracle mindset for today?

_____

_____

_____

Be "bold as a lion." Share the Gospel anywhere,
in land, in the sea or in the air!

DAY 20

THE LADY IN THE WRONG SEAT

*The Spirit of the Lord God has taken control of me!
The Lord has chosen and sent me to tell the oppressed
the good news, to heal the brokenhearted, and to an-
nounce freedom for prisoners and captives.*
ISAIAH 61:1 (CEV)

Before boarding the plane in Davao City, Philippines, I asked God to seat me with someone I could really share Jesus with—someone who needed to hear about God's love and the hope and healing possible when we ask the Lord Jesus to change us from the inside out. I felt a strong prompting in my spirit that He was going to do this in a very big way, and I was excited to see what He had in store. We were in a row of three seats and my mother was on my left but no one was on my right. I looked with great expectation as passengers boarded and took their seats—but no one sat on my right. The flight attendant closed the door and the plane was about to take off, when I silently asked the Lord a question.

*Where is the person, Lord? Surely it cannot be my moth-
er, she has known and loved you for many years.*

The Holy Spirit immediately convicted me with anoth-er strong feeling in my heart.

She's in front of you.

I craned my neck to see over the seat in front of me

but at five feet tall I'm what the kids call, "vertically challenged," and it was impossible. Never one to shy away from the voice of the Spirit, I unbuckled my seatbelt, stood up, and leaned over the seat in front of me where a lady in her late thirties was sitting alone. I gently tapped her right shoulder, and she was understandably startled.

"Excuse me," I said. "But what seat number is on your ticket?"

She checked the folded paper clutched in her hand and said, "23-C."

"Ma'am, you're supposed to sit next to me; this is 23-C." I said, pointing to the aisle seat on my right. She got up and I watched her move slowly—almost robot-like—to the seat next to me. It looked as though she was sleepwalking. She buckled her seatbelt and I introduced my mother and myself as our plane lifted off. When we reached our proper altitude and the plane leveled out, mother wasted no time in falling asleep.

"Where are you going?" I asked my seatmate.

"Cebu City."

I tried to engage her in conversation, but she was clearly uncomfortable and her one-word answers left little opportunity for us to build rapport. I was sure we had never met personally, but it didn't take me long to realize I was intimately familiar with the battle she waged, as her words and actions reminded me of my late husband. David suffered from a debilitating depression that drove him to suicide, and this woman who God clearly wanted me to meet had all the same signs—and then some. My heart suddenly ached for this woman as I realized that my questions were beginning to sound like an inquisition. I'm not one to give up easily, so I cut to the chase and told her the truth.

"I feel God is telling me that I am supposed to talk to you. By any chance, is there anything weighing heavy on your heart today?"

She tilted her head, looked at me strangely, and within seconds her guarded demeanor vanished as she poured her heart out and confirmed my instincts. She was indeed suffering from severe depression and on her way to see a psychiatrist in Cebu City because she was a somewhat prominent figure where she lived in Davao City and didn't want anyone to know she was seeing a psychiatrist. How typical of Satan to use this kind of stigma to keep people from getting the help they need, I thought to myself. We talked about my experience with this illness and what I learned from David and from so many of my relationships with the people we served in Operation Care. I learned that in spite of having a great deal of money and many caring people around her, she felt horribly alone and lost.

"You are not alone," I said, and gently took her hand. "There is real hope in Jesus. He is our healer and comforter. You cannot imagine what a difference He has made in my life—what a difference He can make in your life!"

I was able to share the gospel message with this hurting woman on our hour-long flight and before we landed, this precious lady prayed to accept Jesus as her personal Lord and Savior.

After her prayer she wiped the tears from her eyes and exclaimed. "Now I understand why . . . I understand why . . ."

"Why what?" I asked.

"Why I missed my plane this morning. I wasn't supposed to be on that flight."

"Thank you, Jesus!" I said, not caring if anyone around us heard.

When we landed in Manila, my new sister in Christ decided not to proceed to Cebu City, and declared herself healed—physically and spiritually.

"I'm going to return home on the next flight back," she declared.

It brought me great joy to hear her proclamation, and I felt in my spirit that is where the Lord wanted her to go—that for her, this decision was right. I knew Jesus was thrilled to have His daughter at His side, and the angels in heaven were singing. However, as a nurse I felt it was also important to leave her with some additional words of encouragement. After all, David's faith was strong, but he still succumbed to the utter hopelessness and despair that are the hallmarks of severe depression. It can change and distort the way you see yourself, your life, and even those around you.

"Depression is a very real and very dangerous illness," I said. "In some cases, it is caused by a chemical imbalance that can often be successfully treated with medication and other proactive therapies. If you ever feel hopeless Jesus can give you strength, but He can also give you just the right medical professional to help. Do not feel that you must suffer in silence. Are you sure about not continuing on to see the doctor?"

"I'm very sure, thank you for caring, but I'm still going to return home." She declared, "I don't need to listen to a psychiatrist. I need to listen to Jesus."

"Yes, listening to Jesus is very important," I laughed joyfully as I hugged her good-bye. "After all, it was Jesus who told me you were sitting in the wrong seat!"

MASTERING A MIRACLE MINDSET

It's exciting when we find ourselves in the midst of a miracle, when God blesses us with something miraculous in our life or in the life of a loved one. However, it's even more important for us to realize our unique place in God's grand plan and be aware that we may be the person who God has appointed as the miracle bearer! Think about ways your life touches the lives of others and how you might contribute to someone else's miracle moment.

WHAT IS YOUR MIRACLE MINDSET FOR TODAY?

_____

_____

_____

God's Words are sharper than any two edged-sword.

DAY 21

The Hindu Man and the Bible

For everyone who asks receives, and he who seeks finds,
and to him who knocks it will be opened.
Matthew 7:8

My longtime habit when I board a plane is to pray and ask God to seat me with someone who needs to hear about the Lord. God often has a sense of humor in how He orchestrates these divine appointments. Once, I was on a flight with three other Operation Care team members. The four of us were supposed to have seats together, but God had a better idea. A reservation glitch split us up and placed a software engineer from India between us—a Hindu man named Avinash.

Surrounded by outspoken Christians who love the Lord Jesus, Avinash didn't stand a chance. We introduced ourselves, and when our seat mate innocently asked what was taking us all to India, we gushed with excitement about our ministry trip. By the questions he asked, he seemed genuinely interested in Operation Care. Our plane had barely left the ground when we began to discuss our faith.

"Do you have a god?" I sincerely asked Avinash.

"Yes, Krishna."

"Do you pray to your god?"

"Yes, of course."

"How sure are you that he answers your prayers?"

To this question, there came no ready reply. In fact, the silence that filled the air was deafening.

"Well, let me tell you how my God answers prayer . . . let me tell you about my Jesus . . . " and I began to share my heart with my new Hindu friend.

When I began to quote some Scripture verses from memory, Avinash seemed fascinated—and curious. I was so glad my teammate next to me had a Bible. When I turned to John 3:16 and asked Avinash if he would read the verse aloud, he didn't hesitate.

"For God so loved the world that He gave His one and only Son, that whoever believes in Him shall not perish but have everlasting life."

"Isn't that amazing?" I said, as we discussed what this meant.

"Now, turn to John 14:6," I encouraged him. "Jesus is preparing a place in heaven for us, and He is coming back to get us!" I was so excited to introduce Avinash to God's Word. He was clearly moved as he read John 14:6 and then Romans 6:23 aloud.

"Do you believe in miracles?" I asked.

"I'm not exactly sure what you mean . . . " He tilted his head quizzically.

"You know, miracles—extraordinary events manifesting the supernatural work of God! Miracles are happening around us all the time. We just have to train ourselves to see them—to recognize them for what they are!"

I told him how Operation Care began, and how God had miraculously allowed all of us to travel to different parts of the world and continued to open doors for us to serve the homeless and minister to impoverished children across the globe.

"My life is filled with miracles from God!" I exclaimed. "For example, just before this flight, Jesus helped some of our team members who had trouble with their tickets. It looked like they might not be able to join us, but one miracle after another happened and here we all are!"

"Your faith is—exceptional—encouraging . . . " Avinash smiled and shook his head.

"Think about it!" I said. "The fact you are sitting here between me and my team members is a miracle! This is God's plan!" I could barely contain my joy.

It was a fifteen-hour flight, and we spent a great deal of it talking about Jesus, reading the Bible, and discussing miracles. When the Holy Spirit moved me to ask Avinash if he wanted to experience a miracle and accept Jesus as his Savior, his answer made me want to stand in the aisle and shout with praise and thanksgiving.

"Yes, I do," he said with quiet conviction.

"Then repeat this prayer after me . . . " I said, as the tears rolled down my cheeks. "Lord Jesus, I accept you as my Lord and Savior. Please forgive me of all my sins. Thank you for dying on the cross of Calvary. Please help me in all things; take over my life, and make me a new person in Christ. In Jesus' name. Amen."

As Avinash finished praying, his serious countenance visibly changed and a spirit of soft sweetness came over him. His face is etched on my mind.

Suddenly, I remembered that our chairman of the board gave me three books of John, and I gave one to Avinash. Kelly, a team member, gave him her New Testament Bible.

"Thank you . . . thank you . . . " he said quietly as he accepted the gifts.

What a blessing to experience the moment when the Holy Spirit changes a life. Now, Avinash is a member of God's family.

"God gave all of us a miracle in you, Avinash." I said, as all of us warmly welcomed him into the family of God. "We are all part of His glorious plan, and when we follow Him with unconditional obedience and joy, there is no telling what kind of miracles will happen!"

MASTERING A MIRACLE MINDSET

1. Seeing miracles is all about perspective, about having a willingness to intentionally look for them in everyday occurrences.
2. When you lead a brother or sister to Christ, encourage them to find a church, get a Bible and pray.
3. Then, let God do what God does best. When we plant the seeds of faith, God will take over in the lives of His children and help them grow to fruitfulness and produce a rich harvest.

WHAT IS YOUR MIRACLE MINDSET FOR TODAY?

_____

_____

_____

Unconditional Obedience brings blessings.

DAY 22

Go Back Inside the House!

Wealth and riches are in his house,
and his righteousness endures forever.
Psalm 112:3 (NASB)

It was a lovely sunny day. My heart was bursting with joy and anticipation at the thought of going to Africa, one of my childhood dreams! I barely slept the night before as I prayed about this long-awaited trip where we would be able to help 5,000 children or more in Nairobi, Kenya.

The car was packed, and we were getting ready to leave for the airport. I was already inside the car when a soft voice prompted me to go back inside the house to get a necklace I'd forgotten to pack. At first, I tried to ignore it and told myself I didn't need to take another piece of jewelry to Africa.

Go back inside the house.

This time, the prompting was so strong that I figured I needed to listen and be obedient.

"Okay, okay, I hear You, Lord," I said as I got out of the car. "I guess You must have something special planned if You want to make sure I've got the right accessories," I laughed.

I opened the kitchen door, and as I headed for my bedroom, the phone rang.

"Hello, this is Susie." I said.

"Susie Jennings?"

"Yes …"

"This is Congressman Pete Session's office. We would like to know when you will be in Kenya, so we can coordinate your meeting with our US ambassador."

"The ambassador to Kenya?" I stammered.

"Yes . . . we have your request, and the Congressman asked me to set this up."

I completely forgot that I called Congressman Session's office to ask if he knew how to connect us to Michael Ranneberger, the US ambassador of Kenya, so we could extend a courtesy visit while we were in Africa.

"I'm so happy you called!" I exclaimed. "We are just leaving for the airport now, I came back inside my house to get something when the phone rang—this is a miracle!"

The US Embassy to Kenya opened in 1964. Through our presidentially appointed ambassadors, the Embassy has enriched the ties between the American and Kenyan people and serves the needs of Americans in and around this East African hub. Chief among the US goals are fostering the development of a sound Kenyan economy, strengthening the institutions of Kenyan democracy, helping to prevent the spread of HIV/AIDS, and promoting US/Kenyan business ties. With our team of devoted servants, and a goal to reach over 5,000 children on our trip, we felt it was important that the ambassador knew about Operation Care Africa.

The meeting was scheduled and a few days later on the appointed time, I visited the US Embassy in Kenya accompanied by Pastor Joshua Kagunyi, our partner in Kenya.

"Thank you so much for taking time to meet with us," I

said to Ambassador Ranneberger as we were ushered into his private office. "We have received such a warm welcome by everyone."

During our visit with the ambassador, we could share the overall vision of Operation Care International and why we felt called to bring our outreach to Africa. I gave him our brochure, newsletter, and one of our colorful salvation bracelets. Explaining the meanings of the colors is a wonderful way to share Jesus with someone—especially in sensitive political situations like this.

"The five colors represent the foundations of the Christian faith. Black is for sin; red is the blood of Jesus and His love that wipes away all sin; white is for purity because Jesus died for us, all our sins can be forgiven and washed away; green is for spiritual growth, showing that we will grow as Christians when we read the Word, pray to God, and spend time learning about God with other Christians; and yellow symbolizes Heaven and the streets of gold that wait for us there."

Before we departed, I asked if we could pray for him and the important work he was doing to keep the lines of communication open between our countries. He agreed without hesitation. On that day, I shared Jesus and a prayer from the heart with a powerful man in an equally powerful position, and I could not help but feel humbly grateful that God would choose to use Operation Care and me in such a miraculous way. There is no telling what God will orchestrate when we listen to the still, small voice of the spirit and respond with unconditional obedience and joy. It wasn't a necklace the Lord wanted me to get that day when He sent me back inside my house. He wanted me to get the phone call that led to this meeting—a meeting that I knew in my spirit would lead to something greater—

something only God in His infinite wisdom understood.

On this day, God wanted me to share His words with a United States ambassador inside the hallowed walls of our Embassy in a country hungry for hope and healing. If that isn't a miracle, I don't know what is. To God be the glory!

Mastering a Miracle Mindset

1. What happens when we disobey God's prompting?
2. Obedience protects us from the loss of heavenly rewards. Can you recall any past experiences when you really knew for sure you were obeying God, even when you didn't know why?

WHAT IS YOUR MIRACLE MINDSET FOR TODAY?

_____
_____
_____

My beloved Mom, Betty Yanson.

DAY 23

Anointing with Oil

*Are any of you sick? You should call for the elders of the
church to come and pray over you, anointing you with
oil in the name of the Lord. Such a prayer offered in
faith, will heal the sick and the Lord will make you well.*
JAMES 5:14-15 (NLT)

My mother Betty was eighty-nine years old when she
got shingles, a very painful disease that affects the nerve
endings. The official medical term for this is Herpes Zos-
ter, but it's been called shingles for many years because
of the way the rash blisters overlap one another, like roof
shingles.

Pain is usually the first symptom of shingles. For some,
it can be intense. Depending on the location of the pain,
it can sometimes be mistaken for a symptom of problems
affecting the heart, lungs, or kidneys. Some people experience shingles pain without ever developing the rash.
Most commonly, the shingles rash develops as a stripe of
blisters that wraps around either the left or right side of
your torso. Sometimes the shingles rash occurs around
one eye or on one side of the neck or face. For my mom, it
started on the right side of her forehead with a little spot.

"I don't feel well," she said at first. Then, she began to
experience ever-increasing pain and bouts of numbness
on her face, followed by a period when severe headaches

rendered her unable to function. For one entire week, she woke up screaming in the early hours of the morning because of the excruciating pain in her face. My heart ached for her. When she cried out, I would get up and run into her room with an icepack, give her pain medicine, and stay with her until she drifted back to sleep. It was like an alarm clock that went off every morning for seven days.

Neither of us got much sleep during this time, and it was beginning to take a toll on both of us. I knew it was spiritual warfare because my mother was as much an integral part of the Operation Care ministry as I was, and the enemy wanted us both distracted from doing God's work. It was November, and we were monumentally busy preparing for the annual Operation Care Christmas Party for the homeless, now dubbed by Fox 4 News as "The World's Largest Christmas Party for the Homeless." We usually have over 10,000 people in attendance at the Dallas Convention Center. Since the start of the ministry, my mother was my number-one partner. She lived with me for sixteen years and was my best friend and confidante. In the early days of the ministry, it was Mom who would accompany me to buy countless blankets from dozens of stores throughout the Dallas area. She would push shopping carts loaded with blankets, and for years we spent every Saturday together buying blankets until we became a nonprofit organization in 2001. Without a doubt, she was my number-one encourager and supporter.

Although we no longer scoured local stores for blankets, our ministry responsibilities were still considerable—especially during this busy Christmas season. Plus, in addition to my daily tasks as founder and director of the organization, I continued to work a full-time evening shift job as a recovery room nurse supervisor at Baylor

University Medical Center. I grew accustomed to working sixteen-hour days, but not without sleep. By the seventh day of this shingles nightmare, I was exhausted due to a lack of sleep, and my mother was exhausted from the pain. I didn't know how much more of this either of us could take. That night after she woke up screaming again and when we finally managed to get her pain under control enough so she could drift off to sleep, I cried out to the Lord.

"Jesus! We need help!"

He reminded me of a Scripture in the book of James. "Is anyone among you sick? Let them call the elders of the church to pray over them and anoint them with oil in the name of the Lord. And the prayer offered in faith will make the sick person well; the Lord will raise them up. If they have sinned, they will be forgiven" (James 5:14–15 NIV). Suddenly, the Lord reminded me of something else—something that made me fall upon my knees and beg for forgiveness. Earlier that week, the Lord spoke into my spirit and told me that in addition to my prayers, I needed to anoint Mom and also our house with oil—but at the time I didn't have the energy to do it. I didn't listen to God, and now my sweet mother was paying for my disobedience.

"Forgive me, Lord!" I cried, as I called my dear friend Adelfa Lorilla who is like a sister to me and asked her to specifically pray for Mom and for this horrible disease to depart her body. I asked if she would be able to come to our house immediately and anoint Mother with oil.

"Of course I will." She said. "Give me some time to get ready and I'll be there soon."

I was so glad she was at home when I called. Not long after we hung up, I was surprised to hear the doorbell and see Adelfa and her husband Ricardo standing at the door-step. When I opened the door, they hurried inside.

Then Adelfa said, "As soon as we hung up the phone the Holy Spirit placed a heavy burden on my heart to stop everything I was doing and go immediately to your house with Ricardo." "I didn't even change out of my house dress!"

I practically collapsed into the arms of these loving friends.

"Where is Mommy?" they asked almost in unison. They call my mother "Mommy" because they treat her as their own, something very acceptable in our culture. They followed me to where mother was now sitting on the side of the bed holding an ice pack on her face.

"I could not sleep," she whispered.

"Mommy, we are here to pray for you and anoint you with oil." Adelfa said. "Do you feel well enough to kneel down at the side of your bed?" Ricardo asked. Mother wasted no time in sliding to the floor as these faithful prayer warriors placed their hands on her, spoke powerful words of healing and expectation over her, and anointed her head with oil as the Lord instructed.

After helping my mother back to bed, the three of us began to walk from room to room as we prayed over the whole house and anointed the doors with oil.

"God, we ask You to protect this home and to heal Your humble servant!" Adelfa cried out.

We prayed with all our hearts believing that God would remove any spirit of evil from our house and heal Mom. It was my mother who first placed the seed of a homeless ministry in my heart when I was a child, a heart the Lord would eventually use to start Operation Care many years later. I owed so much to this gentle, loving woman. My mother slept well that night, and for the first time in over a week she did not wake up in excruciating pain. In fact, the headaches stopped completely, and she never had another painful attack. Soon, all evidence of shingles was gone! Thank you, in the mighty name of Jesus! We had experienced the miracle of healing and the power of Scripture, and it convicted me once more of the critical need to always be obedient when the Lord gives instruction—even if you lack the energy—perhaps especially if you lack the energy.

A few years later in December of 2009, Mom went home to be with the Lord shortly before our annual Birthday Party for Jesus. It was a bittersweet celebration that year without her to share it. However, I knew then just as I know now that she will forever celebrate with us in Heaven as the miracle of God's love—and her love—flows from my heart into the hearts of others here and abroad.

MASTERING A MIRACLE MINDSET

The ceremonial act of anointing with oil is often overlooked in today's culture. How can you incorporate this biblical tradition into your worship experience?

WHAT IS YOUR MIRACLE MINDSET FOR TODAY?

_____

_____

_____

*Susie washing the feet of an Indian girl
who came to know the Lord.*

DAY 24

Following in the Footsteps of Jesus

Then Mary took a whole pint of a very expensive per-
fume made of pure nard, poured it on Jesus' feet, and
wiped them with her hair. The sweet smell
of the perfume filled the whole house.
John 12:3 (GNT)

In Biblical times shoes and sandals made from animal skins were difficult to clean and would often become caked in dirt and mud. This is why shoes were typically removed outside of homes and temples before entering. The act of wiping or washing the bare feet of a guest or visitor was a responsibility that usually fell to the lowest house servant. Additionally, having the feet bathed signified the status of an honored guest. Foot washing was considered an honor and became a common Jewish custom at formal banquets.

In the New Testament there are two accounts when the feet of Jesus were washed by women. In John 12:1–3, Mary, the sister of Lazarus washes the feet of Jesus. This takes place at a feast and Mary takes perfumed oil and anoints the feet of Christ before wiping them dry with her hair. In the second account, Luke 7:36–48, a mysterious unnamed women washes His feet with her tears after He dines in the house of Simon, a Pharisee. Like Mary, she also bathes Jesus' feet in perfumed oil and dries them with her hair.

However, at the Last Supper Jesus subverts the ceremony by washing the feet of His disciples. Despite their vocal protests, He reminds His devotees of the significance of foot washing. This action prepared His disciples (and their converts) to walk in the path of righteousness. Jesus makes it very plain that He did not expect from His disciples (or us) something He did not do Himself. Jesus is our perfect example of humility and why our trademark at Operation Care International is foot washing. The following verses are at the heart of why we do what we do.

Now that I, your Lord and Teacher, have washed your feet, you also should wash one another's feet. I have set you an example that you should do as I have done for you. Very truly I tell you, no servant is greater than his master, nor is a messenger greater than the one who sent him. Now that you know these things, you will be blessed if you do them (JOHN 13:14-17 NIV).

Foot washing acts as a renewal of baptism and a commitment to living God's way of life. Foot washing is still practiced in one form or another throughout the world on the Thursday before Good Friday. In Operation Care, it is practiced twice a year; once at our International Summer Outreach held outside of America, and again at our annual Birthday Party for Jesus held at the Dallas Convention Center, a celebration where thousands of God's children come together to experience the magical miracle moments that only God provides.

During one of our Christmas events, there was a volunteer who was reluctant to work at the foot washing area. However, she had brought her young son with her to teach him about service, so when she was assigned to this area she wanted to be a good example to her son even though she did not want to go. She was nervous and could sense the nervousness of the man who sat on the chair at her station—a homeless Vietnam Veteran who was as uncomfortable as she was at first. But with each moist baby wipe she used to gently wipe away the dirt, he began to sense the compassion and genuine love of God exemplified through the volunteer. As he could relax and receive the blessing of being an honored guest, the volunteer also was blessed—and the act changed both their lives. This beautiful exchange was a profound miracle in a sea of miracle moments going on all over the floor of the convention center that day. The power of service to those who the world often deems undeserving is something that offers healing and refreshment to both the receivers and the givers.

This intentional act of radical obedience can be interpreted as Jesus washing away sin as we wash away the dirt and grime from the feet of a homeless person who desperately needs to feel the hope and healing of unconditional love. By this tender act of service, we long for each of our guests to know how special they are to Jesus and to each volunteer who serves during Operation Care Christmas Party. We show them the reason for the season is J-E-S-U-S! Many volunteers are deeply touched as they serve "the least of these," but that year for one volunteer and her young son the experience of being an obedient servant was something unexpected. That day, the miracle was her changed life.

Mastering a Miracle Mindset

Ask God to reveal something to you that He wants you to do that is out of your comfort zone. And then do it.

Part Five

Miracles of God's Provision

Loving volunteers at the "Largest Christmas Party for the Homeless" held at the Dallas Convention Center.

DAY 25

Three Hundred Kids Just Waiting to Sing

And do not forget to do good and to share with others,
for with such sacrifices God is pleased.
Hebrews 13:16 (NIV)

It was late autumn and we were busy preparing to launch Operation Care Christmas Gift 2004, the first Christmas Party for the homeless at the Dallas Convention Center. Everything was falling into place, except for the choir. From the start, I envisioned a huge choir performing on stage, and that year I was certain God was laying it on my heart that it was the Prestonwood Worship Choir. The previous year I had attended a performance of their grand Christmas pageant, and it was that kind of spectacular production I saw in my mind taking place at our event. However, when I called the church in June to invite their adult choir to perform at our event they respectfully declined. Due to the growing success of their annual Christmas production, they were unable to accept engagements outside the church. I was crushed. Surely, this could not be. It was precisely *because* of their extremely elaborate Christmas presentation that I wanted them to participate in our first super-size Christmas party for the homeless.

All summer long I prayed about it, to no avail.

Lord, I know you gave me this vision, please tell me what to do . . .

In the fall I called Prestonwood again, and I was talking to one of their staff about the situation when suddenly through her casual suggestion God responded to my plea.

"Have you asked if the kids could sing instead?" the staff member inquired.

"The kids?"

"Yes, the kids. Prestonwood has a huge Youth Choir," she said, "and they don't perform in the Christmas Pageant."

She gave me the name of the person in charge who could actually make a decision, and I thanked her and hung up the phone to pray. After talking to the Lord and praying for favor, I rehearsed what I was going to say and then picked up the phone and dialed. It only rang twice and I silently thanked God that the lady I needed to speak with was on the other end.

"Hello, this is Jana."

I took a deep breath and launched right in.

"Hello, Jana, this is Susie Jennings from Operation Care. We are planning a huge Christmas Party for the homeless where we plan to share Jesus with thousands of homeless men, women, and children from the Metroplex area. It will be at the Dallas Convention Center on Saturday, December 18 from ten o'clock in the morning until three in the afternoon. We know how powerful the ministry of music can be—especially during Christmas—and we would like to invite the Prestonwood Youth Choir to sing at our Birthday Bash for Jesus."

When I stopped to take a breath I was surprised to hear an excited scream on the other end of the phone.

"You won't believe this!" She exclaimed. "I mean it, you won't believe this! Last summer the kids decided they wanted to sing at homeless shelters during Christmas, and we circled December 18 as a day to do that! We even identified a window of time—from 10 AM to 3 PM! Wait . . . are you serious about this? This isn't a joke . . . ?"

"Of course not! Why would you ask that?"

"Because we didn't think it was going to happen! We've been shot down by every homeless shelter we've approached. None of them have accommodations to hold a choir our size. The kids have been crushed—they felt certain they were being called to sing for the homeless this Christmas but nothing has panned out. We've got 300 kids just waiting to sing and praying that God would open a door."

"Well Jana," I said as I raised my hand in praise and thanked Jesus, "I think He just opened it—how would your 300 kids like to sing at the Dallas Convention Center?"

She was so excited she could barely speak! God had been planning this long before anyone had even formulated a plan or fathomed the event. We had a need and God provided through the Prestonwood Youth Choir. They had a need to sing for this impoverished community and God provided through us. I jumped at an invitation to meet the Youth Leadership Team and speak at their upcoming Youth Meeting to tell them more about what we had planned for our Birthday Bash for Jesus. I was happy to meet so many young people who were so eager to serve. It was a very exciting meeting because we all believed this was God's ultimate plan, and we all felt blessed to be a part of a grand and glorious miracle moment in time.

The momentous day came and 300 on-fire-for-the-Lord

kids poured out of buses and filled the Dallas Convention Center with an unquenchable spirit. They brought gifts for the homeless like coats, toys, and blankets. There was no problem with space as they performed on the largest stage you could imagine. And true to my vision, their voices of praise brought hope, healing, and joy to the hearts of everyone at our celebration. God used their gifts of music and song to change lives that day—including some of their own as He used the experience to shine a light of passion and purpose on several young hearts who felt called into lifetime ministry that day.

After all, when you find yourself in the middle of a God-shaped miracle, is it any wonder that you want to give God the glory for the rest of your life?

Mastering a Miracle Mindset

Has God ever surprised you with a totally amazing reply for a request that you just had to shout with delight? Chances are, that was a miracle moment in your life!

What is your miracle mindset for today?

_____

_____

_____

Susie surrounded by children in Africa.

DAY 26

Feeding the 5,000 in Africa

*And God, who supplies seed for the sower and
bread to eat, will also supply you with all the seed
you need and will make it grow and produce a rich
harvest from your generosity.*
2 Corinthians 9:10 (GNT)

It was the last day of Operation Care Africa, and we
had one final event remaining. Our headquarters was in a
schoolroom in Nairobi, Kenya, and thousands of children
were still waiting outside for help. I feared we would run
out of supplies before we ran out of needy children.

Lord, you did tell me to prepare for 5,000 . . . right?

A Vision Is Born

We were about to leave for our mission outreach
in India in July of 2009 when the Lord placed it on my
heart where our next destination would be. I was excited
to think about Operation Care Africa 2010 because ever
since I was a little girl, I wanted to be a missionary nurse
in Africa. However, if this was indeed God's plan, there
was a lot to accomplish when we returned from India at
the end of July, paramount being to find a contact liaison
in Africa. At this point I had no idea who this could be.
In the fall, God led me to a friend of the ministry who
worked for Campus Crusade for Christ.

"For your outreach to work, you will need someone in Africa who is very well connected," my new friend said. "We have a partnership with Joy Evangelistic Ministries in Kenya and the man in charge of that is coming to Dallas in January with his wife. I will introduce you."

This was good news, but I got even more excited when I heard God's prompting in my spirit about the theme of our outreach.

Feeding the 5,000.

I didn't have a clue where to get the funds to meet the needs of 5,000 children, but when God gives the vision, He gives the provision. I have grown to believe that God will always provide.

LEADERS CATCH THE VISION

When I could meet with Kenyan Pastor Joshua Kagunyi and his wife Tabitha in January, I only had thirty minutes to make my presentation because of a scheduling glitch. I presented them with abundant material about what Operation Care was doing here in the States and then told them about our global vision. I gave them a quick review of our success in the Philippines and India and shared the vision God gave me for Operation Care Africa—Feeding the 5,000.

Pastor Joshua was very quiet while Tabitha asked questions about logistics and provision—particularly the funding required for an outreach of this magnitude.

"We don't have the money yet," I said, "but what we do have is the evangelism program, the logistical plan, and a team ready, willing, and able to carry out the vision. I trust that God will provide the funds." I quickly briefed Tabitha on how we would do the event, and she seemed impressed. I could tell the idea intrigued Pastor Joshua, even though he did his best to remain reserved. They said they would pray, talk with their team in Africa, and get back to me soon.

In February, one of our generous donors gave $5,000 when she heard about Feeding the 5,000.

"And when you go to China, I'll give you $10,000," she said.

We didn't have plans to go to China, at least not yet.

With the donation of $5,000 in seed money, the confirmations I prayed for began to flow one after another—assuring me that we were on the right path. Most of the confirmations came to me in messages and Scripture related to the number five, as in 1 Samuel 17:40, "And he took his stick in his hand and chose for himself *five* smooth stones from the brook, and put them in the shepherd's bag which he had . . . " and later in 1 Samuel 21:3 where it reads, "Now therefore, what do you have in hand? Give me *five* loaves of bread, or whatever can be found." Everything was five, five, five and I was completely sold out to the idea of Feeding the 5,000, and I knew God would provide.

In record time with unprecedented provision, God set the wheels in motion in Kenya with Pastor Joshua and his wife Tabitha, and He provided us generous donations of cash, goods, and services that allowed us to order 5,000 backpacks stuffed with supplies for needy children, including food, shoes, T-shirts, personal-care items, and Bibles.

A Multiplication Miracle

As I looked out at the sea of children's faces, I prayed like never before. Those who were sitting on the grass inside the school grounds were waiting for us to call their name. The children coming to our events here in Africa were all pre-registered. If your name was not on the list, you could not come in. I gazed out at the crowd of young people beyond the school grounds, some with tears streaming down their faces because their names were not on the list. I could picture in my mind the same about Heaven. You would wait outside until your name was called. But if your name was not on the list, you could not come in no matter how much you beg and cry. One of our key Operation Care goals is to make sure everyone's name is on that list and written in God's Book of Life.

We had finished all of our events and were almost at the end of our list of names. As sad as it was to think about the children we could not serve, it was good to know we had made a difference in the lives of so many. When a child heard us call their name, they would leap from the group and run forward, their face beaming with delight as they moved towards the area where we were doing foot washing and introducing them to Jesus. When they left our location, they would proceed to another area where Pastor Joshua and his team were giving away T-shirts, backpacks, salvation bracelets, and food. We just checked off the last name on our list of 5,000 when our driver, Edwin, arrived with the van and tried to rush us out of the slums. We were being hurried (or herded) to the van, when I heard Pastor Joshua calling out to me.

A GOOD PROBLEM

"Susie, we have a problem!" he exclaimed as he ran up to me.

"What problem?" I asked.

"Well, it really is not a problem; it is more like a miracle! We still have supplies to distribute—a lot of supplies!" He grabbed my hand and pulled me toward the room where volunteers had been handing out backpacks filled with supplies to every child whose name was called. We only ordered 5,000 backpacks, and every name on our list of 5,000 was checked off, or a replacement name had been written in the space if no one had come forward, and yet there was still a huge stack of backpacks, shoes, and T-shirts at the back of the room. It almost appeared as though the quantity had not diminished. I stood in amazement.

It broke my heart when I realized we could not meet the needs of all the children who had come to find a glimmer of hope that day. Some of the children were in line for two days, some had AIDS, and many had fevers. Some were orphans, and others were children of the many volunteers who had shown up to help us. Now my heart broke for another reason. God in all His glory had multiplied our supplies, so we could provide a gift of hope to more children.

"Give it to those children who were not on the list," I said to Pastor Joshua. "Children with AIDS, the orphans, the pastor's kids and volunteer's kids, and there are still children standing in line outside waiting and hoping! And some are crying, please give it to them!"

ABOVE AND BEYOND

In what can only be described as a supernatural miracle, God provided supplies for 1,000 more children in dire need, including fifty autistic kids. Our Operation Care team was thrilled to have the opportunity to bless so many additional children, and there was a distinct hush of reverent awe among us as we left the camp that day, for surely, we had been in the presence of God. Our goal was Feeding the 5,000, but when we left Africa, we had met the needs of 6,000 children. And shortly after we returned, God provided an additional unexpected donation that enabled us to fund the building of a school for a Massai tribe in the desert area. Once again, God showed us that He specializes in miracles.

God is—and always will be—more than enough.

Mastering a Miracle Mindset

If we take the time to listen and really look, we can see miracles all around us—in the sunrise, in the flight of a bird, in the giggle of a baby. Miracles come in all shapes and sizes, including super-size ones that can take your breath away. Grab a piece of paper and write down the most profound miracle you can recall in your life. Put today's date on it, fold it in half, and place it inside your Bible.

What is your miracle mindset for today?

_____

_____

_____

Birthday party in South Dallas, a partnership with First Baptist Church, Dallas, TX.

DAY 27

$28,000? JUST CHARGE IT!

I will stand at my watch and station myself on the ram-
parts; I will look to see what he will say to me,...
HABAKKUK 2:1 (NIV)

It's been years, but I can still recall the conversation I had that September day in 2003 when Ron Creswell, one of the pastors at my church, called.

"Susie, have you ever heard of the Edie Clark Annual Christmas Party that is held every year in the projects?"

"I'm not sure . . . " I replied, as I searched my brain to recall what I knew about the event, which turned out to be nothing.

"Every year Edie Clark gave a Christmas party for kids who live in the three Dallas projects: the Turner Courts, the Frazier Courts, and the Rhoads Terrace Court. These are low-income areas where the families live on $16,000 a year or less," Ron said. "Edie Clark spearheaded the party, and every year she organized, hosted, and funded it. She's a longtime member of First Baptist—or *was* a longtime member—she just passed away."

I was sorry to hear that, but I didn't know Edie and couldn't recall ever meeting her.

"Susie, can Operation Care help plan and organize this

party?"

"Ron, we're a homeless ministry; you realize that, right? We're not a children's ministry."

"I know, but we're talking about 5,000 kids who probably won't have any kind of Christmas at all if this doesn't happen."

Oh my goodness, 5,000 children, Lord?

I love children. I come from a big family of nine kids, and Ron knew I obviously loved children because I taught the preschool class in Sunday School at church. But 5,000? That was most certainly a horse of an entirely different color. As I talked more about this with Ron, it soon became evident that we were being asked not only to replace Edie Clark's organization and hosting tasks, but her financial contribution as well—which at this point was an uncertain figure. Our entire annual budget for our blanket ministry is only $10,000, and our board is a fiscally responsible entity—I wasn't sure how they would take to my idea of even approaching them about the topic. However, I began to hear the voice of the Holy Spirit.

You need to help these kids.

"Ron, I need to pray about this, but I will take your request to our Board of Directors immediately."

"Susie, I figured you would say that, and there is a representative from the City of Dallas who is in charge of the Rhoads Terrace who would like to meet with you and your board to tell you more about the party. I will be happy to come with her; would you meet with us?" Ron asked.

"Let me call the board members, and I will call you right back."

Spirit-filled Conviction

Because of the deep conviction the Holy Spirit placed

in my heart, I asked the board to consider the request. So, they agreed to meet with Ron Creswell and the representative from the City of Dallas.

It was the second week in September when we met. If we agreed to do this, time was running short. After introductions, the city representative launched right in.

"Edie Clark was a widow who devoted herself to these kids. She was a nurse with a caring heart. She was a small woman in stature, only five feet tall, but she had a big personality."

"It sounds like she's describing you, Susie," one of our board members said.

I had to agree. The similarities were astounding . . . *widow, nurse, short, and a big personality.*

"I brought some photos of Edie from the last Christmas party." She laid them out on the table for us to see.

"I know her!" I said. "She attended the 11:00 AM worship service and always sat with a young man in the same pew with me!"

"That is her son," Ron said. "I was surprised when you said that you never met Edie, you were both so very much alike," he added.

A Green Light to Go

After thoroughly discussing the event and the need, the board agreed that although it was out of our ministry scope, we would nonetheless accept the responsibility—with the help of First Baptist Church. Things moved quickly after that. There was no time to lose. We had never coordinated such a huge event. It required a great deal of organization and logistical planning. Fortunately, there were a lot of records from past events, and our liaison with the city and the leadership of Dr. Mac Brunson from First

Baptist helped considerably. At the time, our blanket out-reach into the streets every year at Christmas was our only event. In retrospect, we all agree that God was giving us valuable on-the-job training for the mega-size events He had planned for the future outreach of Operation Care!

There was only one problem—and it was a big prob-lem. We didn't have the funds. We needed 5,000 Christian books for kids, 5,000 Rainbow Faith bears (an evangelis-tic stuffed toy with different colors all over its body), and 5,000 "Finding Nemo" gospel tracts, based on a hit movie that year. Operation Care was still planning our annual Birthday Bash for Jesus to be held one week before the Edie Clark Annual Christmas Party, and we needed to buy 1,000 blankets.

After researching the cost, I discovered we would need $28,000 more.

God Answered Quickly

Lord, where are we going to get that kind of money?

It was then I heard that familiar voice in my spirit.

Pay it yourself with your credit card.

I did not question God as I picked up the phone and began to call the members of our board.

"I'm going to pay this expense with my credit card. I understand Edie's heart, and I believe God has called us to be her heart this year. These children may not be home-less, but they are needy. And they especially need the true gift of Christmas—Jesus."

I never lost sleep over my decision. I knew God want-ed that party, so we could share His love to the kids and their parents. I had no idea where the money would come from to pay for the charges, but I obeyed and placed the order for what we needed. Philippians 4:19 became my treasured verse, "And my God shall supply all your needs according to his riches in glory in Christ Jesus" (NIV). When God calls, we need to listen and obey because when He promises—He delivers! In fact, it was just a couple of weeks later God provided us with $38,000—enough to pay for the charges on my credit card and cover our $10,000 blanket budget.

History in the Making

On December 13, 2003, we conducted our annual Birthday Bash for Jesus when we flooded the streets in Downtown Dallas with volunteers and went under bridges to give away 1,000 blankets to our homeless friends. We had no idea that in a few years we would be conducting our annual party at the Dallas Convention Center for almost 10,000 homeless men, women and impoverished children. The following week on December 20, 2003, the City of Dallas closed a street near Rhoades Terrace Recreation Center, so we could host the Edie Clark Annual Christmas Party. The Dallas Police Department provided officers to help. We had puppet shows, face painting, a balloon artist, clowns, and free food. It was like being at a carnival. First Baptist Church provided about 500 joyful volunteers who were eager to be a part of this celebration. This group of amazing volunteers exhibited the love of Jesus in such an authentic way that it inspired everyone that day!

Thousands of kids and their families had a great Christmas that year. Even more stupendous, 153 accepted Jesus as Lord, most of them were kids. God used us to bring the miracle of salvation to those kids. There is no telling how many lives—and future generations will be changed because of those decisions. From the similarities I had with Edie Clark to the monetary provision, God made His plan and purpose clear every step of the way. My job was to listen—and obey. I'm so blessed that I got to experience those miracles out of obedience.

I'm so glad God gave me the opportunity to say, "$28,000? No problem, charge it!" And I'm so glad God paid it!

Mastering a Miracle Mindset

1. What is the most difficult decision you've made (or didn't make) when it comes to being obedient to God?
2. How does unconditional obedience tie in with God providing miracles in our life?

What is your miracle mindset for today?

_____

_____

_____

President Joel Allison (in suit) along with my co-workers expressing joy before blessing me with a prayer.

DAY 28

A Miracle of Obedience

*For we are God's handiwork, created in
Christ Jesus to do good works, which God
prepared in advance for us to do.*
Ephesians 2:10 (NIV)

There are seasons in life that become turning points when we are changed forever. The Bible says, "There is an appointed time for everything. And there is a time for every event under heaven" (Eccl. 3:1, NASB). Timing is something that has always been important to me because I think it's important to God. Moving forward, going backward, or staying put, it's all about timing. Discerning what is really God's will versus what is our own stubborn or disobedient nature is a never-ending quest in life, don't you agree?

Sometimes His will for us is clear; other times, not so much. When God spoke to me that fall day in 1993 shortly after my husband died and told me to go under the Canton Street Bridge and give blankets to the homeless, timing was a critical thing. I had asked God what I could do. He responded. Then, it was up to me to listen and obey or pretend I was clueless and wait for another time when I could obey or ignore God. I chose to trust and obey God, and He set into motion an amazing journey that I could never have imagined in my wildest dreams.

Operation Care grew from a blanket ministry in the streets of Dallas to an International mission outreach spanning the globe. The more I listened with an expectant heart and responded with unconditional obedience the more the ministry grew. However, there was still one issue simmering on the back burner of my life—an issue that was beginning to cause me to question if I truly believed in God's provision. I had been working as a nurse for thirty-three years, with the past twenty-eight at Baylor University Medical Center in Dallas. As a supervisor in the Recovery Room, I made a hearty six-figure income, and my benefits were more than a blessing. And I truly loved being a nurse—helping people. But no matter how I sliced it, my work as a nurse had become a "job" and the time I spent in ministry at Operation Care was my true "calling." I was born to be a missionary who helps homeless and impoverished people fall in love with Jesus.

Praying for Wisdom

A decade of juggling two full-time responsibilities was beginning to take its toll. As the outreach grew so did the responsibilities. The only way I could get everything accomplished was to sleep less—that was the only portion of my day left to adjust—but I knew that wasn't a wise choice in the long run. In all my years with Operation Care, I had never drawn a salary—in fact, I often supported the ministry with my personal income. The debate to leave my nursing job was one I had grown accustomed to having with myself, especially on my morning prayer walks. And I imagine the Lord was getting a tad tired of hearing my excuse-riddled pro and con talks.

Lord, I'm too young to retire. If I leave now I will lose my retirement benefits. But if I stay, I will lose my health. Lord, how will I support myself without a steady income? You always provide funds for our outreach missions, is it time to ask You to provide a salary for me?

On and on it went like this—for years.

A Season of Change

Then one day a miracle happened. Suddenly, God revealed the answer to me. Not through His voice or the prompting of the Holy Spirit, but through the wisdom of an elderly man who wasn't afraid to speak his mind. Sometimes we know the answer to a difficult question deep in our heart and soul, but the key we need to unlock the epiphanies are the words spoken by someone else. God often uses people to manifest miracles in our life. To help us see clearly that which has hovered in the background in a hazy confusion. That's what happened to me.

One day, I was meeting with two Operation Care sponsors—a mission-minded husband and wife whose support I appreciated and faith I admired. I was practically bouncing off the walls with excitement as I shared all the miracles that occurred on our recent trip to Africa, and the plans we had for future international mission trips. I gave them an update of events we were in the process of coordinating, as well as ideas we were considering.

"We had no idea the magnitude of your outreach!" the wife said.

Her husband asked about my work at Baylor and how I managed to juggle so many responsibilities, and I unintentionally deflected the question by sharing how miraculously God had provided in Africa.

"God is so, so good!" I exclaimed. "He has a plan, and I cannot wait to see what He will do next!"

I noticed they had grown quiet. I thought they were shaking their heads in amazement at what we were accomplishing, but I was wrong.

"Susie, why are you still working as a nurse?" the husband asked.

His question took me by surprise.

"Uh … because it's my job …," I stammered.

"You do know that people quit jobs all the time," he said.

"But then I wouldn't get my retirement … and I have expenses… and bills to pay… and Operation Care doesn't have the money to pay employees . . . and . . . I stopped rambling when I realized that my excuses were beginning to sound like complaints.

He looked at me, tilted his head, and made a comment that had a profound impact on my life.

TENDER WORDS OF TRUTH

"Susie, you were born to share Jesus. You could spend another ten years at your job as a nurse, but I guarantee if you do that, you will look back and regret that you didn't resign now and go out into the mission field."

I let his words sink in.

"You talk about miracles all the time, Susie. Look at what God has already done in your life. Don't you think you can trust Him to provide for you?"

That conversation led to a radical shift in my distorted thinking, and almost in the blink of an eye God provided a miraculous answer to some of the financial worries that had kept me in bondage. He helped me see the big picture more clearly than I had in years. I resigned from my job as a nurse in early January of 2011. My precious co-workers in the Recovery Room gave me a party that

John McWhorter, the CEO of Baylor attended. On January 14, my hospital friends gave me a lovely farewell party on the seventeenth floor of Baylor University Medical Center. Joel Allison, the president of Baylor University Medical Center, and Chris York, the vice president attended. Many of the guests prayed for me, led by Dr. Don Sewell, the director of the Faith in Action Initiatives. I loved my co-workers and my work at Baylor, but now God was calling me to serve in a much different way. All of the gracious good-byes left me emotional, but deep inside my spirit was soaring.

A Long Time Coming

There was no need for transition time, and the last day of my work as a nurse coincided with the first day I became a full-time employee of Operation Care International, almost eighteen years after God called me to go under that bridge. Gone are my retirement benefits. Gone is the six-figure income. Gone is the safety net of supervisor seniority, and gone is the inner battle that waged inside my heart—a battle that the enemy was only too happy to use against me when it suited his needs. Today I am living a new chapter in my life. Today I am proud to shout, "I am a FROG person!"—a _F_ully _R_elying _O_n _G_od person.

As with many missionaries, I live day-to-day dependent on God's provision. And I serve a God who is utterly and completely dependable. I am forever grateful to that faithful servant of God who challenged me to focus on the work laid before me.

Jesus was in earthly ministry for thirty-three years when He went to Heaven. I was a nurse for thirty-three years when I discovered heaven on earth and went into full-time ministry. I believe I will always be a nurse—it is part of who I am. Now, I'm just taking care of people in different ways. The time I spent in the nursing profession has helped me become the person I am today—God used those years to prepare me for a new facet of the caring profession. Like many, I felt called to be a nurse, but then God called me to a different place. He called me to a homeless ministry to serve the "least of these." And I will go where God sends me, all for His glory and honor and praise.

What a journey it has been! It's exciting to see the handprint of the Lord. I suppose I could say one of the greatest miracles I've experienced is my own transformation. I've made a covenant with God to trust Him in all things: to listen for His still, small voice and, when I hear it, to respond with unconditional obedience. And during those times when His message is murky or my mind is shouting too loud for my heart to hear, I'm going to trust Him to send people into my life who can help me filter out the minutiae and focus on the miracles.

MASTERING A MIRACLE MINDSET

1. Is there something holding you back from being a FROG person?
2. What does being more obedient to God mean to you?
3. Write down ways God has shown you His provision.

WHAT IS YOUR MIRACLE MINDSET FOR TODAY?

_____

_____

_____

Guests standing in line outside the Dallas Convention Center for our annual Birthday Party for Jesus.

DAY 29

Paid in Full – Tetelestai

So do not worry, saying, "What shall we eat?" or "What shall we drink?" or "What shall we wear?" For the pagans run after all these things, and your heavenly Father knows that you need them.
Matthew 6:31-32 (NIV)

We just finished another annual super-size Christmas Party for the homeless at the Dallas Convention Center where we were once again able to reach out to over 10,000 people. We provided them with socks, shoes, coats, personal-care items, sleeping bags, blankets, food, medical assessments, entertainment, praise and worship, free telephone calls, and the availability of other resources for the homeless to get help. It was a very special day where memories were made and lives were changed. Operation Care has a main mission to evangelize, to share Jesus with everyone we serve. This event gives us an opportunity to reach thousands of individuals and share the greatest gift of all—the gift of our Lord and Savior—the One whose birthday we celebrate—J-E-S-U-S!

Our trained volunteers talk to our homeless guests one-on-one about Jesus and His love for them, and if the guests give their permission, they pray for them. What began as a street-wide blanket distribution ministry in 1993 has now grown into an evangelistic outreach of miraculous magnitude. We are blessed to have generous sponsors and donors; however our expenses for this event are considerable. This particular year they were exceptionally high. After the event, we needed to pay the bills. Our desire has always been to pay outstanding debt as soon as we can. This is especially important for end of the year events when we want our year-end financial records to be up-to-date. However, I had to pray hard because this year our debt far exceeded the amount we had budgeted.

Lord, I know you have a plan. Please help us.

Three days after the event, I got a phone call from one of our donors.

"So, how did the Christmas party go?" he asked.

"It was wonderful!" I exclaimed. "We had over 10,000 people come through! We are so thankful to the Lord for everything!" I proceeded to tell him about some of the highlights of the day, and it was exciting to relive the experience that was still fresh in my mind and heart. It truly was a miraculous experience for so many people.

"So, what about your funds?" He casually inquired.

I was surprised at the question. I seldom get a phone call from a donor casually asking about funds *after* an event. This is usually a question asked beforehand.

"Uh . . . what do you mean?" I asked.

"I mean, how are your funds? Do you have enough money to pay your bills?"

"No, sir, we don't," I sighed. "I'm sitting here now with invoices in front of me trying to figure out exactly what we owe and praying about which bills to pay first."

"Well, pay all that you can and then call and let me know the remaining balance."

"Okay," I said, wondering if I should take this to mean that he would help in some way with the balance or perhaps direct me toward someone who could. It was a rather ambiguous request, but I'm the obedient servant and I did as I was asked.

I tallied up the expenses and paid what I could, but the remaining balance was still considerable. I shook my head and picked up the phone.

"We still owe . . . " When I told him the balance I didn't know what to expect.

"Susie, I am sending a check today for the entire balance."

Suddenly, our remaining debt disappeared. It was instantly paid in full! No questions asked. Who does something like that?

Jesus, that's who!

Tetelestai– Paid in Full!

Mastering a Miracle Mindset

Tetelestai is the Greek word meaning, it is finished, or paid in full. What does this mean to you?

What is your miracle mindset for today?

_____

_____

_____

A joyous send off to New York for Donna and children.

DAY 30

A Mother's Journey Home

*The Lord will protect you from all danger;
he will keep you safe. He will protect you as
you come and go now and forever.*
Psalm 121:7-8 (GNT)

In March of 2012, Donna's husband abandoned her and their three children because of domestic problems. Soon they were evicted from their home. With only the clothes on their backs and what few personal items they could carry, Donna and the three kids—Joel (age 9), Carl (age 7) and Nicole (age 2)—entered the streets of Dallas to find shelter. They soon discovered the family shelters were frequently full and found themselves spending long nights camping in the park. Donna used bandanas as tethers to tie her children to herself, fearing they might be snatched from her as they all slept at night. During the day, as the two older children were in school, she and the youngest child would go into a local grocery store where Donna would steal food to feed her family. Things got so desperate that she even went to the extent of "selling" herself to survive.

As winter approached, she and the children were able to get into the Salvation Army Shelter program, but Donna knew they could only be free from this terrible situation if they could return to New York and her family. She contacted dozens of local churches, begging for travel assistance but got little to no help. Then one day, a pastor told her about Operation Care and gave her my contact number. It was a few days before our big annual Christmas party for the homeless when she and I spoke briefly on the phone. At that time, I didn't know the extent of her situation, but I invited her and her family to Operation Christmas Gift at the Dallas Convention Center. With renewed hope, she and the kids came to the event.

Unfortunately, she was unable to locate me personally and felt uncomfortable asking someone to find me when there were so many people just like her filling the Convention Center.

Although Donna left the party that day with the same worries, she had a renewed faith that God would help her get home, protect her children, and survive the nightmare she was living. The love of Jesus that filled the celebration was now filling her heart and spirit with hope.

A Hopeful Heart

The next day she reached out to me once more. After hearing her full story, I was the one bawling on the phone. By now, this precious woman was numb to the horror and tragedy she had experienced—her only thought was to protect her children.

"My mother-in-law lives in New York. She will take care of the children, so I can work and find us a place to live. We must get back there . . . Please, can you help us?"

I knew God had brought her to us and I promised her what He was laying on my heart.

"Donna, we will help you—we will get you and your children home before Christmas!"

She cried as she gave me her mother-in-law's phone number and when I called her, she was almost screaming with joy when I told her we were going to send Donna and her three kids home via the Greyhound Bus. She assured me they could stay with her and was ecstatic with the news that her grandchildren would be home for Christmas. Within the next forty-eight hours, God moved two other Operation Care board members and three volunteers to make sure that this homeless mother-of-three made it home to New York. On December 18, 2012, six volunteers stood with the family and prayed before they boarded the bus bound for Rochester, New York. With heartfelt prayers, some pocket money, snacks, and Christmas gifts, we sent them off on their journey home.

ANSWERED PRAYER

Prior to our December event, I specifically asked God to allow us to make a powerful difference in someone's life that Christmas season. I asked God to reveal to me in a very clear way just how the ministry of Operation Care is helping to transform lives, and this was the answer He gave me! Donna said it was a miracle for her and the children to be able to get safely back home. However, it was also a miracle for me. In allowing us to be instrumental in this homecoming story, God responded to my prayers. I called a few weeks later to follow up, and Donna's mother-in-law told me that the two older children were enrolled in school a few days after they arrived in New York, that Donna and the kids were already in an apartment that she helped them get, and that Donna was looking for a job.

Once Donna got back home, this mother was able to get some family support nearby to help her. However, this is a success story that all too often doesn't happen when a family is thrust into homelessness. Our shelters and resources are predominantly set up to address the needs of individuals. For the most part, our work at Operation Care is to address the urgent physical needs of the homeless and the critical spiritual needs. However, as God's plan for us continues to unfold, our ability to advocate on behalf of this population grows, as does our involvement in the bigger picture solution to the problem.

We serve an awesome God. And our deepest desire is to bring Him glory and honor in the way we serve those in need. Please help us to protect them. Will you be a part of the solution? For ways you can help us make a difference in someone's life today, please see the information on the "How You Can Help" page at the back of this book.

MASTERING A MIRACLE MINDSET

There are times when a helping hand can literally help save a life. Never underestimate your ability to change the life of someone in need. Please pray about ways you can help Operation Care provide miracles to homeless men, women, children and families, just like Donna's. Visit us at our website today, or send me an email at sjennings@opcare.org.

WHAT IS YOUR MIRACLE MINDSET FOR TODAY?

_____

_____

_____

Susie experiencing homeless life firsthand.

DAY 31

My Night on the Street

The Lord is my light and my salvation:
Whom shall I fear?
Psalm 27:1 NASB

It was a beautiful bright October afternoon when I stopped by the Day Resource Center in downtown Dallas to visit with my homeless friends. The Center is a kind of "safe haven" where the homeless can stay during the day before they go back out into the night. In the evening, some go to homeless shelters to sleep, if there is an available bed, and others will return to the streets where shelter is found under bridges, near dumpsters, in alley's or in abandoned buildings.

At the Day Resource Center, the homeless can shower, get assistance with physical and mental health care needs, and talk with caring individuals who are professional social workers or volunteers.

That day, I met a homeless couple at the Center who needed a ride to one of the local shelters about 1.5 miles away. I offered to take them. On the way to the car, another homeless lady whom I befriended in the past came running towards me.

"Susie, Susie! I'm happy to see you! I want to help, what

are you doing today?"

As the Founder and President of Operation Care, a ministry to help the homeless with their physical and spiritual needs, I'm often on the streets distributing blankets, personal-care products, food, handing out tracts, and praying with people. Many times we have volunteers assist us—some from within the homeless community. This was a woman who had helped us in the past, and we had developed a friendship.

"Thank you, Sally, but we're not handing anything out today. I'm just leaving to take this couple to another shelter."

"Oh, can I go with you? I can help direct you, I know where all the local shelters are …"

I had been to every shelter in the DFW area more times than I could count over the years, but feeling useful is important to people in Sally's situation, so I accepted the offer graciously.

On the short drive, I learned the couple were just transient, and hoped to leave the next day. They were very appreciative they did not have to walk to the shelter. After dropping them off, I had some time and invited Sally to lunch before I took her back to the Center where she asked to be dropped off, she wanted to take a shower and get cleaned up.

It was perplexing to me—the life she lived—and although my years in this ministry and in nursing afforded me an understanding about the complexities in the lives of the homeless population, I still couldn't quite grasp the reality of her life.

She was chatting away, and I was looking for a place to stop and get a bite to eat when I heard the voice of the Lord speak to my heart.

Susie, you are going to become homeless for a day.

For a moment, the thought of it shocked me. Then I quickly began to see God's wisdom. He wanted to give me a closer glimpse of how the homeless actually lived so I will have a better understanding of their way of life.

My mind began to run a mile a minute at how I was going to do this, and in retrospect I can see where my next decision might have been hasty—impulsive. I told Sally.

"I think God wants me to be homeless for a day. To see what it's like," I said.

"That will be good!" She shouted. "We can pretend we are old friends and I will show you around. I will show you the best places to get food, and the safest places to sleep, and we can even tell the Dallas Morning News, and they can document your being homeless on the streets of Dallas! And ...."

I partially listened to her rapid-fire ideas as I grabbed my phone and called Ron Batts, the chairman of our board. I knew he was out of town in Cleveland, but I had to share this brilliant idea from God with him. He was a bit nonchalant at first, but soon he could see the value in the experience. When I hung up, Sally was still talking about all the things we could do, riotously rattling off suggestions.

We stopped for a sandwich and talked more about the plan.

Her mind was going even faster than my own, and before I knew it I got caught up in the moment—like I was planning an undercover adventure with this "insider" as my ally.

We talked about what kind of clothes I would need, what I should take with me, and how to disguise myself, since I was well recognized in the homeless community.

"I know of a place where you can get a wig!" She exclaimed. "It's downtown, I pass by it all the time. I could get one for you!"

What was I thinking when I gave her $40 to go buy one for me?

The plan was to do this in three weeks. I was still working my full-time evening shift job as a nurse supervisor in the Recovery Room of Baylor University Medical Center, and that would give me enough time to prepare mentally, emotionally, physically and spiritually.

THE PLOT THICKENS

Over the next few weeks, I would meet with Sally to discuss my plans. She showed me a downtown church where they allowed the homeless to sleep in the outdoor parking lot adjacent to their enclosed parking structure where a security guard was always on duty. After my evening shift at 11:00 PM, I would often go to the church and bring her food and clothing. Soon I was bringing sandwiches to hand out—a lot of sandwiches—there were so many people who slept in this parking lot.

I was drawn to the homeless young people who slept on the opposite part of the lot away from the adults. When I discovered that several of them had upcoming birthdays, I gave them a surprise birthday party with the help of the security guard. One night I brought balloons, ice cream and cake after my evening shift, and we celebrated inside the enclosed structure, an area strictly off-limits to the homeless community but with the guard's help one that afforded us a unique opportunity for a private party—something several of these young folks had never experienced.

As we got closer to the day of my "undercover operation," I began to see a change in Sally. Every time I asked if she bought my wig, she would give me another excuse, like she left it in the church or a friend was holding it. It was always something. I ended up buying a wig on my own and stopped asking her. Clearly, she spent the $40 on something else.

After spending time with her these past few weeks, I suspected the "something else" was drugs. I could see all the signs, including seriously erratic behavior.

How could I have been so foolish?

We were on our way to get a hamburger one day when I confronted her inside my car. Big mistake.

"Sally, can I ask you a question?" I said quietly.

"Sure."

"Are you taking drugs?"

I shouldn't have been surprised by her vehement reaction, but in looking back I can see it was one of the many experiences the Lord would use to give me not only a deeper understanding of the complex nature of homeless people, but a deeper understanding of myself, my motives, and my expectations. It is good to be sensitive and caring, to treat the homeless with compassion and love. But it is also important not to be naive and enabling—it's sometimes difficult to know where to set healthy boundaries in these relationships.

I wanted so much not to be judgmental, but I was learning that I still had some lessons to learn. As much as I wanted to think of Sally as a friend who was just down on her luck and had a few bad breaks, that wasn't all there was to it. There was a bigger picture—and when she began to scream at me and wave her arms around wildly, I began to see just how big that picture was.

"Who the h**l do you think you are accusing me of taking drugs?" She screamed into my face. "You're just like everybody else thinkin' that we homeless are all on drugs! What right do you have comin' in here and getting' all up in my stuff and tellin' me I'm a no account drug addict? Huh? Tell me… go on, tell me …"

Her voice was catapulting around the interior of my car like ricocheting bullets, and I was so scared. No one ever screamed at me that way in all my life. I was afraid she was going to hit me.

"I'm sorry, Sally! I'm sorry," I cried. "I was wrong, I made a mistake! Please forgive me!" I had to calm her down, and I apologized profusely for wrongly judging her and I told her I would never ask her that foolish question again. I began to look at our relationship differently after that—and I prayed for wisdom to understand how God really wanted me to help her.

THE DAY ARRIVES

On a cool Friday in November, I donned my wig and put on a very old tattered T-shirt and gray pants, and slung a cloth tote over my shoulder where I had my pen, camera, phone, wallet and notebook—but no money.

I asked my close prayer partners to pray for me, and on the way to downtown I asked God to shield me and direct my steps—to show me what He wanted me to learn from this experience.

I parked my car inside the church parking structure adjacent to the lot where the homeless slept, thinking that would be my place to sleep that night also. I had just exited the building and was walking down the street when I met one of the homeless men I had befriended.

"I know you!" He said. "What are you doing here, why are you dressed like that?"

So much for my disguise.

"Shhhhh…" I looked around to see if anyone was close. "God told me to be homeless for a day!"

He looked at me strangely but said he would help me.

Suddenly, I could see Sally walking fast towards me, she appeared very upset. She ignored the fact I was in "disguise," and seemed oblivious to our agreement that she would not divulge my real identity.

"Susie, I need a ride to the Resource Center."

It was more of a demand than a request. When I told her I was unable to help, I was fearful how she would react. When she began to get irate, the man moved protectively between us, and Sally stormed off. I quickly learned that extremely erratic behavior and sudden episodes of violence is commonplace on the streets—and something you need to always be prepared for.

"You shouldn't be out here," he said, as we walked. "It isn't safe for girls."

I thanked him for his concern and assured him I would be okay before I crossed the street to join three of the homeless teenagers I had also befriended. They knew of my plan, and I felt protected that day as we walked and walked for hours around downtown. The young people carried all their worldly belongings as they roamed the streets, laughing along the way. They were decidedly more carefree than the homeless adult population.

Young people are most often homeless because they have run away from an unpleasant—and sometimes dangerous environment. Some are rebellious and angry, others are lost and confused. Many have escaped into a world of drugs. Some are in the streets because their parents kicked them out, some came from jail.

I think it was easier to show them the love of God because even though their lives were monumentally messy, their hearts didn't seem as hardened by the world in which they were living—not yet. They seemed willing to hear what I had to say about Jesus, and I felt they respected why I was out there among them.

"I think God wants me to know what this really feels like," I said sincerely.

What it mostly felt like, during the daylight hours at least, was aimless.

I was profoundly affected by two significant things— the first was the complete lack of any purpose or direction, other than focusing on where to go for food and clothing, and waiting in line to get it. The second and far more disturbing feeling was that I had become invisible—and as such I was no longer deserving of kindness or respect. As we walked, people often crossed the street to avoid us, or looked away as our paths crossed. Eye contact was virtually non-existent and even the most basic of social interaction was avoided. I made it a point to say "hello" to everyone I passed and few would even acknowledge my existence, let alone respond in kind.

"I've lost my home—not my humanity!" I wanted to shout.

THE NIGHTMARE OF NIGHTFALL

When evening came we walked back to the Day Resource Center. The sidewalk stank of urine as we sat on the curb near the smelly trashcan and talked about life on the street.

Suddenly, the sound of my growling stomach startled me.

"Church people usually come by to feed us," one of the young men said, while the others made mooing sounds like cattle.

"Is that what you feel like when they bring food?" I asked. "Like animals?"

"Sometimes," they said.

At 8:00 PM, a local ministry that regularly brought food to the homeless came. I recognized the founder and hid my face. Were it not for the generosity of countless volunteers and church members, many of the homeless would go hungry for days. Some volunteers came in groups and distributed food on foot, talking one-on-one with the men, women and young people. Others would stay in their vehicles and hand out food and supplies from the window or from the back of a truck.

Seeing this reminded me of a story I heard from a friend who volunteers with her church to distribute food. She was in the passenger side of a vehicle one day.

"At one point, a large group of homeless adults surrounded our truck, everyone was reaching hungrily to get food when the two people in the back of the truck began to throw wrapped sandwiches and small bags of chips into the crowd. I'm sure their intentions were good, but it was dehumanizing to watch, and when some young folks standing nearby began to make sounds like cattle and pigs being fed at a trough, it broke my heart."

When she told me this story, I agreed with her, no human being should be treated like an animal and throwing food was unacceptable.

Fortunately, no one tossed food at us that night.

After dinner, clothing was given away, and I gave the red flannel skirt with a matching red scarf I got to a homeless teenage girl.

Then it was time to go to sleep. We walked back toward the church parking lot but my group of young friends stopped by the church stairs.

"We sleep here now," one of them said.

"Not inside the parking lot?" I asked.

"Nah, those old folks are bad news," another said, "it ain't safe with them."

Sleeping on the stairs next to the road didn't feel safe to me. I'd heard stories of cruel people who drive by late at night and throw bottles and trash at homeless people sleeping on the street. I decided to take my chances in the parking lot with the adult homeless, where at least there was a portable potty and a security guard.

SHADOWS OF SADNESS

I said good-bye to the kids and walked alone toward the crowd of adults who were claiming their territory for the night. Everyone was busy putting down cardboard pallets and sleeping bags, and positioning their handcarts, shopping carts, and plastic trash bags filled with belongings around them. I quickly learned that preparing for sleep is a major production.

I'd never felt more vulnerable. Men clearly outnumbered women. While I knew that being homeless did not automatically mean you were a violent criminal, it was quickly apparent that by this time in the evening many of the people around me were now under the influence of alcohol and drugs, and under those conditions might do things they normally wouldn't.

It was all so very sad, seeing the pain, frustration and loneliness on so many faces. I had "head knowledge" about the reality of the vicious cycle of alcoholism and drug addiction, but now God was opening the eyes of my heart to see the "need to be numb" from an entirely different perspective.

I never thought I'd say it, but after only one day of wandering aimlessly and feeling like discarded trash, I could better understand the choice to drown out the hopeless feelings of desperation in any way possible. But the medication these precious souls needed was the unconditional love of Jesus!

If only they knew how precious they are to You, Jesus! If only they felt like sons and daughters of a King, with an eternal treasure in Heaven! And not like cast off diseased cattle. Lord, how can we really reach them? How can we really make a difference in their lives?

I was praying fervently and walking slowly when I practically ran into Sally. I prepared myself for another angry outburst, but she acted as though the altercation earlier that day never occurred. It was like she was a different person.

"Looks like you need somewhere to sleep," she said. "You can stay here with us."

A Place to Lay My Head

The "us" was with her and her new boyfriend. I wasn't convinced this was my best option, but as I looked around I figured it would be safer to lie down next to someone I knew rather than a complete stranger. Plus, I really liked Sally. When we first met I found her quite fascinating, and we had developed a fast friendship. However, she was changing and her sudden anger and erratic behavior frightened me.

"Come on, let me show you how it's done," she said.

Together we located cardboard boxes from the dumpster nearby to place under my sleeping bag. She helped me set up a space next to her and her boyfriend's sleeping area in the corner of the lot.

I crawled into my sleeping bag and even through several layers of cardboard the cement was hard and cold under my back on that November night. I looked around me and I was scared but I also knew that God called me to be there.

Lord, please protect all of us here tonight.

There were about one-hundred men and women scattered about. Some had sleeping bags, some slept only on cardboard. Some had blankets, some did not, and many shared one blanket between two people. In almost no time, Sally and her boyfriend were sound asleep and snoring loudly.

There were unfamiliar sounds all around me, and I could not sleep. I quietly got up, and I was walking along the edge of the lot when the security guard noticed me.

"I remember you," he said. "You're that birthday party lady; you don't belong here."

"Does anyone belong here?" I said sadly, as I told him why I was there.

"Are you hanging out with her?" He pointed toward Sally's sleeping area, and I nodded.

"You do know she's a major crack head, right?" He didn't wait for a response. "Serious druggies like her don't usually last too long out here, and she's about as serious as they get. She's manipulative, controlling and really dangerous. Trust me, lady, you need to get away from her, she's trouble with a capital "T.""

I had suspected Sally was on drugs, and I guess a part of me just didn't want to believe it, but hearing it from the security guard was confirmation.

"God has called me to this place, and He will protect me," I said.

"That's good to hear, but just so you know, I'm gonna watch your back, too," he said.

It was around 12:30 AM when a group of young people came by to give away sandwiches and pray. They noticed me as a "new homeless," and we started to talk when one of them recognized me.

"You look familiar, didn't I meet you a few weeks ago when you were dropping off some food and clothes for one of the women out here?"

I told them who I was and that God spoke to my heart to live on the street for a day.

"He wants me to really know what it feels like to be homeless," I whispered.

"So, how does it feel?" they asked.

"It feels like I've disappeared—like I don't exist as a person because I'm homeless. It's like I lost my home and the right to be treated with human decency at the same time. It feels very...lonely."

They understood. We talked about our experiences sharing Jesus with the homeless and for a while, they became light in that very dark place. We agreed that the best thing we could do was to show pure and simple unconditional love—to plant the seeds of Jesus in the hearts of the homeless and let Him do the rest.

Before they left, we held hands and formed a circle in that parking lot as they prayed for me with the homeless sleeping around us. I assured them I would be okay, that in addition to God Almighty, the security guard on duty was watching out for me.

An Unspeakable Evil

I was exhausted and needed to sleep. When I left my sleeping bag, Sally was snoring so loudly that surely she must be in even deeper REM sleep now, I thought. Perhaps I could slip quietly back into my sleeping bag and rest my eyes for a bit.

I stopped to use the portable potty, and it was beyond disgusting, but I had no choice.

When I got back to my sleeping area, Sally's boyfriend was still asleep, but she was gone.

I looked around and didn't see her. Fear gripped me, especially now that I knew she was a serious drug addict. What if she turned on me again and got violent? What if she convinced one of the bigger men to teach me a lesson by hurting me? I began to think of all the horrible things someone could do to me, and I was genuinely frightened. My chest was tight, and I was having palpitations. Suddenly, out of the corner of my eye, I saw movement in the distance. It was Sally. I scurried into my sleeping bag and pretended I was asleep, praying that she hadn't seen me.

I laid there completely still for what seemed like hours, but was most likely only a few moments when I heard Sally walk past me. After a few minutes, I opened my eyes just a tiny bit, and I could see her sitting on the ground, her back against the church wall. She looked agitated as she picked at the hem of her sweater. Then, I saw her look up and smile broadly just as I felt something brush against my forehead.

I still didn't move, but the exhaustion in my body was suddenly replaced with deep foreboding as I peered through slivers to see a tall dark man approach Sally. He wore a long black leather coat, and I surmised that is what I felt against my face as he walked past me. It was already the dark of night but this man brought even more darkness with him. It felt like Satan himself was standing just a few feet away. I couldn't hear what they said, but then he handed her something. Clearly, I was watching a drug deal take place.

I shut my eyes tight and started quoting scriptures in my head.

No weapon against me shall prosper! He who is in me is greater than he who is in the world! The Lord is my shepherd, I...

After the man departed, I could hear Sally rustling around, followed by the unmistakable click of a butane lighter. I was afraid to even peek from under my lashes but I assumed she was most likely using the drugs she had just received. It physically hurt to think of Sally caught in the grip of addiction. It was incomprehensible to imagine how she—and all of these precious souls managed to survive this lifestyle night after night. The pictures in my mind of the homeless men and women sleeping around me caused a deep sadness in my spirit. My heart ached in a way I never thought possible.

The Lord kept me safe over the next few hours as I laid there quoting Bible verses and praying. I shivered from the cold, and my bones ached from the hard concrete, but I was afraid to move. I was afraid to encounter Sally in her current state, but I prayed fervently for her. I stayed awake all night, intensely aware of how vulnerable I was—how vulnerable everyone in that parking lot was.

At 5:15 AM, the security guard came around and began calling out.

"Time to get up folks...time to get up..."

At last, morning had broken! I was very grateful for the day light. I had never been so scared in my life. When I sat up, I could see Sally and her boyfriend still asleep. I didn't waste another minute thinking about the fearful night and quickly gathered my sleeping bag as quietly as possible, discarded my boxes in the dumpster and briskly walked from the lot toward where my car was parked.

Before I could reach my car, Sally came running after me—screaming.

Her garbled words didn't make sense, and I realized this wasn't the Sally I once knew; it was the drugs talking. It was heart-breaking to see her in that condition, but there was nothing I could do for her at that moment except pray and follow the security guard's advice and get away from her. I ran to my car and sped out of the lot.

Thank You, Jesus, thank You, Jesus, thank You, Jesus... I said over and over as I drove home.

A Changed Life

When I followed God's call to be homeless for one night, I never expected it to have such a profound impact on me—to change me so completely. I'm ashamed to say that at first I looked at it as somewhat of an adventure—but that perspective changed quickly after only a few hours on the street.

In just 24-hours, my life could have changed drastically, had I really found myself catapulted into homelessness. The desperation and fear create an immediate downward spiral, and once caught in this cycle it's very difficult—although not impossible—to get out. Nothing is impossible with God, and I believe that with all of my heart.

I learned that it's easy for many of us to judge the homeless community—to wonder why they aren't doing more to change their circumstances—why they aren't taking full advantage of all the resources now available to help them. God showed me the answer to that question.

It isn't about the tangible resources available—the blankets, food, clothing, and shelters. Yes, those things are indeed helpful and kind, and Proverbs 19:17 reads, "Whoever is kind to the poor lends to the LORD, and he will reward them for what they have done" (NIV).

What it's really all about comes down to the intangible miracles of love, identity, and self-respect. No amount of stuff can ever fill the God-shaped place in our heart except God. The best way to help our homeless brothers and sisters break this vicious cycle is to introduce them to Jesus, show them the Jesus in us, and let Jesus change them from the inside out.

God's Word tells us that "...We love because He first loved us" (1 John 4:19 NIV).

Our job isn't to try to fix, change, or enable our homeless friends—our job is to plant the seeds of Jesus' love in their hearts and let God strengthen their spirits with Holy Spirit guidance.

I never saw Sally again after that night, I heard she moved to another city. My prayer is that the seeds I planted will one day grow in her heart.

What is the miracle in this experience? A changed and better me!

The Bible says in 2 Thessalonians 2:16—17, "May our Lord Jesus Christ himself and God our Father, who loved us and in his grace gave us unfailing courage and a firm hope, encourage you and strengthen you to always do and say what is good."

Our homeless community is hungry and thirsty for human contact and unconditional love and respect. That's really the best—and the most caring thing we can give.

We can provide blankets, shoes and socks to keep them physically warm for a season—and we can provide the Living Water of Jesus love to keep them spiritually warm for a lifetime.

A physician once said the best medicine for humans is love. Someone asked him, "What if it doesn't work?" He smiled and said, "Increase the dose."

Please join me in offering the Lord our unconditional obedience as together we provide the Food that can change hearts and lives. Let's take this journey together and increase the dose of love wherever God calls us to make a difference for Him.

"Because he loves me," says the LORD, "I will rescue him; I will protect him, for he acknowledges my name" (Psalm 91:14 NIV)".

MASTERING A MIRACLE MINDSET

How can you exercise radical obedience and show Jesus' love today to someone who feels unloved or unlovable?

WHAT IS YOUR MIRACLE MINDSET FOR TODAY?

_____

_____

_____

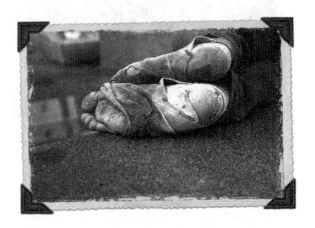

IN CLOSING

DEVELOPING A HEART OF J-O-Y

Let your eyes look straight ahead,
fix your gaze directly before you.
PROVERBS 4:25

As each miracle story unfolded on the page, a new one would come to mind. In a lifetime of miracles, it was challenging to select just thirty-one to share with you in this, my first book. I never knew the process of writing and publishing a book could be both difficult and delightful. However, what I did know was that when God has His fingerprints on a project, the wisest thing we can do is listen to His voice and obey. Writing this book has been quite an experience for me.

I hope you've enjoyed this glimpse into my Operation Care journey over the past few years. My prayer is that in sharing these miracle moments with you, I can encourage you to walk in your passion and purpose, and to live the life of joy I have discovered. My life of ministry and the Operation Care mission are woven together. Fulfilling my mission in the world is God's plan and purpose for my life. I love how this Scripture verse exemplifies this, "The most important thing is that I complete my mission, the work that the Lord Jesus gave me" (Acts 20:24, NCV).

Being able to fulfill His plan and purpose is all about listening for His voice and exercising unconditional obedience when God speaks. Please let me clarify something, when I say, "I heard God's voice," I'm not necessarily saying that an audible voice spoke to me, although that has occurred. For the most part, when God speaks to me, He does it in very creative ways in my heart, mind, spirit, and soul. I've spent a lifetime learning to tune into God's voice. It's a spiritual discipline that you can learn, too. I believe you can also learn how to see miracles in your life more clearly.

In biblical times, those who doubted that Jesus was the Messiah, would frequently goad Him into proving it by serving up a miracle. "Then some of the Pharisees and teachers of the law said to him, "Teacher, we want to see a miraculous sign from you" (Matt. 12:38). They often treated Him like a short-order cook, "Hey, Jesus, give us some of your wisdom and a side order of miracles."

It doesn't work that way. Miracles by definition are extraordinary events manifesting a supernatural work of God—an unusual event, thing, or accomplishment, a wonder, a marvel.

We cannot simply ask God to "show" us miracles. What we must ask is for God to change us over the course of our life and shape our heart to allow us to experience these miraculous moments in time, to "see" them with our physical eyes and the eyes of our heart. And when we see them—for surely we all have—what then do we do?

What does it take for us to allow God's miracles to really change us? To actually cause us to grow, believe, depend, share, witness, and devote our life to the One who provides them?

It takes faith. And spiritual discipline—exercise.

As a nurse, I understand the value of physical exercise. It's important to keep the temple God has given us healthy and hearty in order to do the work He has called us to do. As a Christian who deeply loves my Lord and Savior, I also understand the value of spiritual exercise, the need to develop a healthy and growing relationship with Jesus. That is why I combine the two and begin most every day with what I call a "prayer walk" around my neighborhood. I've been doing this for many years. It's when I talk to God, think through the issues of my day with Him, and ask for His wisdom, guidance, and yes . . . sometimes I even ask Him for a sign.

Then, I go home and almost always read from Psalms or Proverbs. Occasionally, I open my Bible randomly and allow God to teach and guide me through His Word. It is amazing—downright miraculous even—how He opens the eyes of my heart during these times! This is how I have grown to love my Jesus. Every miracle depends 100 percent on our relationship to God the Father, Jesus the Son, and the Holy Spirit.

When Jesus was miraculously walking on water, He enabled Peter to do the same, but when Peter took his eyes off Jesus, he became frightened and sank into the water. So it is with us. When we fix our eyes on Jesus, we can stand tall and walk firmly on any shifting sand in life. We can all master a miracle mindset and train ourselves to see God in everything.

I've learned so many things as God has accompanied me on this journey of life. My relationship with the Lord is the most important in my life. It is the constant nourishment I need and the solid foundation on which I stand. My goal is to encourage you to look at your life in terms of miracle moments: to help you train yourself to listen for

God's voice and follow His wisdom and guidance with unconditional obedience. That is when true joy can be yours.

True joy comes when we can prioritize what is truly important in life.

J = Jesus

O = Others

Y = Yourself

Since leaving my full-time job as a registered nurse, I've been blessed with the ability to go into this ministry full-time. As a little girl, I dreamed of missionary work. And today, that little-girl heart lives on inside me and I think that perhaps God has called me to be a missionary of miracles.

Let me encourage you to not only see the miracles in your life, but to master a miracle mindset that will enable you to grow closer to God, listen for His voice, and offer the unconditional obedience that will in turn manifest these miracles in your life in a supernatural way. It is through His provision that miracles can and do happen.

In all things to God be the glory and until the next time, I remain yours . . .

In His service until He comes,

Susie

PS: I'd like to say something about the person who helped me give birth to *31 Days of Mountaintop Miracles*. Allison Bottke, is a miracle herself. She is so passionate about her work, and she believed in this project with all her heart. Allison is a very gifted professional writer and editor, and has been extremely patient with me, a novice in this field. With her guidance and attention to detail, I finished writing this book in twenty-three days—amazing!

Her ability to organize, edit and prepare the manuscript for printing is another miracle. Even our final cover design is based on her original concept. I could never ask for a more perfect partner in this God-appointed time and project. He brought Allison to help me bring the incredible stories of my miracles to life. I will be forever grateful—thank You, Jesus—and thank you, Allison!

Allison and me when I gave my keynote talk at the Fellowship of Professional Women luncheon in December 2010.

At the OCI Gala fundraiser
September 2014 - Dallas, TX.

About Susie Y. Jennings, RN

Author and Founder of Operation Care International

Susie arrived in the United States in September of 1982 from her home in the Philippines. Within a few months, she joined First Baptist Church Dallas where she received invaluable biblical knowledge under the teaching of the legendary Dr. W.A. Criswell. Susie taught preschoolers for twenty years at her church, where she remains a member to this day.

Desiring to serve God and her community after the tragic death of her husband, God called Susie to give blankets to the homeless in downtown Dallas in November 1993. The homeless call her, "The Blanket Lady." That modest beginning was the genesis of Operation Care International, which has grown to encompass multiple ministries and major events each year in Dallas, Texas as well as missions to the homeless and destitute children in nations around the world.

A registered nurse by profession since 1978, in obedience to God's calling Susie stepped out in faith and resigned from a supervisory position at Baylor University Medical Center Dallas in January 2011; thus becoming a full time missionary to those in need.

Her guiding principle for the vision of Operation Care International comes from Romans 8:28, "And we know that God causes all things to work together for good to those who love God, to those who are called according to His purpose."

Susie's life Bible verse is Proverbs 3:5-6, "Trust in the LORD with all your heart and do not lean on your own understanding. In all your ways acknowledge Him, and He will make your paths straight."

Susie Jennings continues to lead Operation Care International with the help of a board of directors and a multitude of volunteers. This is her first book.

You can reach Susie Jennings through her website at
opcare.org
or on Facebook at
Facebook.com/susie.jennings

About Allison Bottke

Allison Bottke is an award-winning, best selling inspirational author of thirty published nonfiction and fiction books, including the acclaimed *Setting Boundaries*® series from Harvest House Publishers. *Setting Boundaries with your Adult Children,* has hit #1 in the amazon.com "Parenting" category several times, and is still heralded as a landmark resource for parents and grandparents. *Setting Boundaries with Food* won the prestigious Selah Award for Best Book of the year in 2013. She is also the founder and general editor of over a dozen volumes in the popular *God Allows U-Turns*® anthology.

Allison also has a passion to help writers achieve their dreams, and she has served on the faculty at many national writing conferences, such as Jerry B. Jenkins Writing for the Soul, Blue Ridge Christian Writers, Roaring Lambs Christian Writers, Seattle Pacific, and others. She has maintained over a decade-long active and thriving presence online with multiple websites and blogs, and stays current with trends in marketing and publishing.

Allison has a passion to work with results-oriented people who want to turn their writing and publishing dreams into reality. She works one-on-one with a limited number of clients every year and offers ghostwriting, developmental editing, and substantive editing services.

You can reach Allison Bottke through her website at SettingBoundariesBooks.com

Our Mission:

Operation Care International exists to glorify God. In obedience to His will, we connect impoverished children and the homeless to Jesus Christ by providing for their physical needs through God's provisions both at home and abroad.

About Operation Care International

Born of a widow's grief in 1993, Operation Care International became an official nonprofit ministry in 2001 and is dedicated to caring for the homeless in Dallas, Texas and impoverished children around the world.

Since November 1993, when founder Susie Jennings and a group of volunteers distributed 100 new blankets to the homeless living under the Canton Street bridge overpass in downtown Dallas, Operation Care has been faithful in carrying the message of love and hope to those in need through the power of the Gospel of Jesus Christ.

As of 2014, Operation Care International has conducted major outreach efforts in nine countries, including; the Philippines, India, Africa, Taiwan/China, Indonesia, Cambodia, Jordan, and Israel.

Operation Care International has also enjoyed a long-time partnership with the Union Gospel Mission where one evening a month we provide a volunteer team and a minister to lead a worship service and pray with the homeless men after the service. Afterwards we serve them dinner at the Dining Hall.

God has placed a vision in the heart of Susie Jennings to celebrate the birth of Jesus Christ in cities across the nation to provide a place where the homeless and the outcasts of society will be the special guests. Visit the Operation Care International website at **opcare.org** to find out more information on how your community can participate in **America Celebrates Jesus 2020.**

opcare.org

Our Expanding Mission

In addition to yearly international events, the mission of Operation Care International has expanded to encompass several major charitable events each year in the Dallas Metroplex area. Each event generally has a theme:

- The spring event, which celebrates Easter, provides personal-care products, clothing, Bibles and gospel tracts to individuals at shelters or on the streets.

- At summer events, bottled water (labeled with the message of hope), personal-care products, Bibles and gospel tracts are distributed.

- For Thanksgiving, as the weather turns cooler, we deliver clothing, personal-care products, Bibles and gospel tracts.

- We close out our calendar of events with the nation's largest Christmas party for those in need, held at the Dallas Convention Center every year since 2004. Each year in December, thousands of volunteers come together and thousands of people form lines early in the morning for this special event.

Who are the homeless?
40% of men are veterans
42% are children under age six
15% have college degrees
45% are women and children
100% need your help

10th Annual Christmas Gift 2013

Event Highlights

- 300,000 sq. ft. at the Dallas Convention Center

- Over 8,500+ homeless and impoverished guests served

- 3,300 volunteers representing 300 churches, multiple organizations and corporations

- 11,900+ meals served

- 234 pallets of coats, clothes, shoes, socks, blankets, sleeping bags, personal items, and toys

- 6,294 pairs of new shoes distributed

- Over 1,200 sleeping bags, 2,500 blankets and 4,500 children's and adult coats distributed

- 32 different groups provided praise and worship music

- Countless lives were changed

Visit the Operation Care International website at opcare.org to find out more.

How You Can Help

Many of the miracles I've shared with you in *31 Days of Mountaintop Miracles* were made possible by gracious donors and sponsors that felt called to contribute to Operation Care. By listening to God and offering unconditional obedience, their generosity has changed the lives of countless individuals and even future generations. If God is laying it on your heart to help, we thank you in advance for acting on that prompting. No contribution is too small that God cannot multiply it in miraculous ways.

Operation Care is a 501(c)3 nonprofit organization. Your donation is tax deductible as allowed by law. Operation Care is a member of the Evangelical Council for Financial Accountability (ECFA), an accreditation agency to promote fiscal integrity and sound financial practices among member organizations. You can trust our stewardship of your gifts.

We also welcome inquiries from you or your financial planner concerning opportunities to fulfill your philanthropic mission, including charitable gifts, annuities, or bequests.

Susie Jennings is available to speak on the topic:
Unconditional Obedience: The Key to God's Miracles

Contact Us:
Operation Care International
P.O. Box 224136
Dallas, TX 75222-4136
Phone: 972-681-3567
Website: opcare.org
eMail: info@opcare.org

A Legacy of Gifted Professionals

Since 2001, Operation Care International has thrived under the leadership of many gifted individuals. Our volunteer board members give generously of their time and talents. We thank the following professionals for their service over the years on our Board of Directors.

* = Founding Board Member

Kay Almquist, Christina Armstrong, Martha Batts, Ron Batts, Alex Bustamante, Pilar Bustamante, Stan Cole, Mike Congrove, Lisa Cooper, Chris Courtney, Gary Daniels, John Davis, ***Manel Diwa**, Connie Dunkin, Elizabeth Farris, Julie Grayson, Imelda Gutierrez, Al Hewitt, Tony Higuera, ***Susie Jennings**, Wilfred Job, Gladys Jones, Kerry Knott, John Lay, Cecilia Lujauco, Kandace Lindsey, Diana Lyons, Michelle Maroon, Naphis Mitchell, Johnny Murray, Jose Pastrana, Don Perritt, Marie Reed, Heather Roberts, Richard Sanders, ***Nena Schnitman,** Ginny Sills, Shari Snyder, Rebecca Tanner, Nancy Thomas, Roel Van Eck, Janet Ward, Michelle Welch, and Jim Willmon.

God Bless You One and All!

The cover photo for this book was taken especially for this project, and the location has a very special significance in my life.

In the Introduction, I shared the moment with you when my missing husband was no longer missing—when our search team discovered David's earthly body. This is near the location in Atoka, Oklahoma where my life was forever changed.

I will always miss my precious husband. Yet I know that he is rejoicing in heaven, and I lift my arms in praise that God used David's tragic death to give birth to an international ministry that has changed countless lives. It took one life so others may live! Sometimes, miracles come in unexpected ways.

It's difficult to think that David had to die in order for my compassionate heart to live. However, that is the painful truth. It was through the tragedy of loss and the pain of confusion that caused me to cry out in desperate obedience to God.

Today, I am serving the homeless and impoverished, people I did not like in a ministry I did not want.

And I cannot think of any other way to live—I have to obey unconditionally.

To God be all the glory, honor and praise.

Thank You, Jesus, for specializing in miracles!

ANNUAL BIRTHDAY PARTY FOR JESUS
Guests of Honor: Homeless and Impoverished Children

Haircuts

Medical

Food

ANNUAL BIRTHDAY PARTY FOR JESUS
Guests of Honor: Homeless and Impoverished Children

Foot washing

Vision

Prayer/Evangelism

ANNUAL BIRTHDAY PARTY FOR JESUS
Guests of Honor: Homeless and Impoverished Children

Blankets/Sleeping Bags

3,300 Volunteers

Honoring the Homeless vets and WWII Heroes

Annual Birthday Party for Jesus
Guests of Honor: Homeless and Impoverished Children

Praise and Worship Team/Entertainment

International Summer Outreach: (July)

2008 Philippines
(2,000)

2009 India
(2,000)

2010 Africa (6,000)

2011 Taiwan (2,700))

2011 China (20)

2012 Indonesia (4,000)

2013 Cambodia (3,000)

2014 Jordan (1,800)

2014 Israel (1,300)

All proceeds from this book will go to
Operation Care International.

Each time you purchase this book, YOU are helping the
homeless and impoverished children here and abroad.

Pray, Volunteer and Give.
Visit www.opcare.org

"He who is kind to the poor lends to the Lord."
PROVERBS 19:17

Imagine, lending to the King of kings
and the Lord of lords!